God

Makes

No

Mistakes

By

Jane McCaskill

Xulon
PRESS

God Makes No Mistakes
by Jane McCaskill

Printed in the United States of America

ISBN 978-1-60477-863-2

Unless otherwise indicated, Bible quotations are taken from The New Scofield Reference Edition of the Bible, Copyright © 1967 by Oxford University Press, Inc., and Life Application Study Bible, The New International Version, Copyright © 1988, 1989, 1990, 1991, 1993, 1999 by Tyndale House Publisher, Inc. Carol Stream, Illinois and Zondervan Grand Rapids, Michigan.

www.xulonpress.com

To my friend, Shirley.
May God's richest blessing
fall upon you and be
blessed forever.

Love
Jane McCaskill
Jerm. 29:11

To My Wonderful Husband,

Thank you for making my life full of excitement and fulfilling. I would not want to imagine what path I would have taken without you. You have been unselfish, kind and have lavished your love on me much more than I could have ever asked for. When I did not believe in myself, you were there to encourage me and to hold my hand. You saw a beauty within me when I could see no beauty. You have never sought your own, envied nothing and are not easily provoked. You have suffered great patience with me and have bore all things as my partner in life. No evil have you uttered. You have believed in all things, hoped in all things and endured all things. Truly your love has never failed me. This life's journey has been amazing as we have walked hand in hand and shared our sorrows, trials and great joys together. I rejoice with you that our marriage has been a blessing and I thank God for bringing us together in His perfect plan. Thank you for your love for Him and for serving Him. I love you with all my heart and soul.

Jane

FOREWARD

~:~

My husband and I spent two terms in Italy as mission-aries. During this time I saw the hand of God move in countless ways. I praise Him that we had the opportunity to serve Him in that capacity and to have the exposure of living outside America. We, along with our children, have a greater appreciation for our country, even with its faults.

I have been a Christian for thirty-six years. It has been an adventure I shall never forget. He has brought me through trials time and time again and each time I have grown. I have faced adversity and fear only to have Him calm the storm and walk on the water and come to me. He has miraculously answered prayers and accomplished extraordinary things to make a way for me when there was no way.

God's existence is a certainty in my life. It is evident to me that He sits on the throne of my heart. I love Him and I want everyone I meet to see how wonderful and magnificent He really is. I can only sum it up in a song:

I worship you Almighty, God,
There is none like You,
I worship you, oh Prince of Peace,
That is all I want to do!
I give you praise,

For you are my Righteousness! (I have none of my own)
I worship you, Almighty God,
There is none Like You!

This book is an actual account of events in my life. From my perspective there were many times where my focus was not properly directed. I have had much to learn through the years about God's grace and provisions. Often I had to learn the hard way, through trial and error. I am still not perfect and never expect to be. Life is a learning process and graduation is still in the distance. I would like to say that I am proceeding and by God's grace making fewer and fewer mistakes. We all have a path to take in this life. Our choices along the way, good and bad, make us more and more like our Lord Jesus Christ.

I have chosen to reveal myself, with my faults, my failures, and my victories for you to see my humanity. We are all in the same boat with our sins, our shame, our past our failures, our futures and hopes. God can still use us and teach us truths about Himself. He delights in giving us the desires of our heart. He wants us to have faith in Him. He desires our fellowship. He answers when we call on Him. My prayer is that you will see Him at work in my life as you read the pages in this book. I know He can work in you as well.

ACKNOWLEDGEMENTS

I acknowledge that many people have contributed to my writing this book but I am truly indebted to my parents. I miss them so much and look forward to the day when I shall meet them again in glory. Mom, Dad, I love you. Thank you for your prayers and encouragement through life and making this book possible.

My greatest blessings in this life have been you girls. I am so proud to have been the recipient of you; my lovely daughters, Amanda Lynn, Brooke Tyler, and Kelly Elizabeth. You are a tremendous encouragement and support to me. I love each of you from the depths of my heart. May God bless you as He has blessed me!

Thanks to Kristen Roels, my daughter's roommate and friend, who spent her time to the editing this book.

I am indebted to Sarah Stump, my life-long friend and sister in Christ, who not only proofread but gave me valuable insight and suggestions. Thank you Sarah for your support and prayers as you edited and wrote the book cover. I will always count it a joy and privilege to have been your friend for life! I could not have done this without your help!

To the Reader:

As you read my personal experiences with the God of the Universe, my prayer is that you will realize that God is uniquely involved in each of our lives. We need to acknowledge that God is in control as we see His divine plan and His divine hand in our lives. Nothing is by chance in the Christian's life. God has a plan for each of us. We can either seek Him and His direction, or we can choose to ignore His presence and walk in disobedience. Climb into my time machine and go back with me and take a good look at how God can work in a girl, a woman, a daughter, a mother and a wife.

TABLE OF CONTENTS

CHAPTER I

MEMORIES NOT FORGOTTEN

⁓:⁓

Deuteronomy 4:9 *Only take heed to thyself, and keep thy soul diligently, lest thou forget the things which thine eyes have seen, and lest they depart from thy heart all the days of thy life; but teach them to thy sons, and thy sons' sons;*

The day had finally arrived. I had been waiting what seemed like a life time for this very moment. I was twenty-seven years old and thought that I had missed out on the very thing every girl wanted out of life....Marriage. But here I was bouquet in hand, about to walk the isle in my newly bought white gown. I was the happiest woman alive. My heart pounded hard as my father walked me calmly to the entrance of the sanctuary. "A Time For Us" started on cue and I stepped forward with many doubts. "Am I making a mistake? Do I really love this man?" As I glanced to the front of the sanctuary, there at the altar, waiting to take me as his wife was a sensitive, wonderful man. God put a calm assurance in my heart and I knew this was His plan for me, for us. But what lay ahead was a journey I had not antic-ipated in this lifetime. Settling down and having children would be a normal existence I had expected. However, God took us where we did not plan to go and on a path that was not easy to say the least.

The first eleven years of my life, my parents and my sister and I lived with my grandmother and her youngest son. Uncle Buddy had been shot in the leg when he was sixteen and had many emotional problems. My grandmother was like a mother to me. She sheltered me and calmed my fears and tears. My parents worked hard and the day finally came that they could launch out with their family and purchase a house. They had waited for many years to be able to afford a house of their own. Dad worked two jobs most of the time trying to provide and save some money. Our home was very modest, two bedrooms and one small bath. The yard was very nice with shade trees and plenty of room to run and play. My dad planted a garden and mom canned green beans, squash, beets and tomatoes in the summers.

My parents loved my sister and me and we knew that! My mother was only sixteen when she married and had me nine months later, my sister coming nineteen months later. We all sort-of grew up together. They always had plenty of time for us. We took vacations together and enjoyed camping quite a few times during the year. They enjoyed camping as much as anyone I had ever seen. Dad built our first camping trailer. He called it "Dreams End". It was somewhat dangerous though; dad did not know that trailers needed an equalizer hitch to keep them from jack-knifing back then. It's a wonder we never had any incidents with the trailer. I can still feel it swaying on the road as we would zoom pass tractor trailer trucks every year that we headed for the beach at four o'clock in the morning.

My teen years were difficult to say the least. I was an obese child and adolescent. I had not even started my menstrual cycle at the age of sixteen. (Which I now know was due to polycystic ovaries.) I was developing many masculine characteristics. My hips were narrow and my shoulders were broad. I had too much hair on my arms and face. I could not control my eating and I received constant criticism from my father who could not accept an overweight child. My mom had scared me to death of boys when she told me what they were capable of and told me "never let a boy touch you". She told my sister the same things but somehow I ended up with a phobia about boys. I was scared to death to be near one.

When I was twelve I begin taking diet pills a local doctor prescribed. They really worked but I was working myself to death with the high I was getting. I cleaned and ironed and cooked, while my sister occupied herself with the TV. Every summer I would take those pills but my weight was like a roller-coaster and I never seemed to get a grip on how to loose weight and keep it off. All I knew was that I was hungry all the time and unless I took those pills I gained weight. Little did I know at the time that those pills were a drug called speed, well abused in the 60's and 70's.

Being overweight had an effect on me in several ways. It gave me a severe inferiority complex, a lack of security, it filled me with self-pity and I had no confidence. To enhance all those qualities, my peers called me names and teased me about being overweight. My sister on the other hand was "daddy's little girl". She did not have a weight problem. I remember him doting on her and getting her up for a snack of peanut butter, bananas and crackers after they had put us to bed. When I asked for some, I was told, "No, you are too fat, you can't have any". My grandmother, with whom we lived at the time, would sneak around to the other door of the bedroom and give me some candy and say "here honey, grandmother loves you." My parents meant well.....they thought that giving me a late night snack would make me gain more weight. Grandmother did not intend to set me up for self-pity, and being a child I could not understand what was happening to me. That was when the roots of self-pity took hold and the association with love and acceptance was blurred with the hurt feelings. The food my grandmother provided made me feel comforted and loved, I suppose.

When I was five years old, Dr. S. Charles, our pastor, had come to our house and told my parents that I had come forward in Vacation Bible School and had made a profession of faith and that I needed to be baptized. They kept insisting and I did not want to disappoint anyone even though I did not remember the whole ordeal of going forward. Shortly there-after, I remember going into the baptistery with water up to my neck and being baptized. I was scared to death of water so right before I went under I gasped for air and several folks chuckled. I grew up in a Baptist church and went to revivals, Sunday morning worship, teen summer camp and even sang in the teen choir. I had always been moral, never let a boy touch me, never drank or ran in wrong crowds.

When I was a teenager, everyone I knew smoked. It was not considered a sin since R.J. Reynolds Tobacco Co. was the industry that put Winston-Salem on the map, food on the tables, clothes on our backs and built many churches through out the Piedmont. Both my parents worked there, most of my relatives and a host of people in the church. On Sundays men gathered outside the church doors and smoked between services. So it was no surprise or disappointment to my parents when my sister and I took up the habit in our early teens.

Dating during those years when girls had to be kissed by the age of sixteen didn't look too promising for me. I really wanted to date like all the other girls and my sister, but I was never asked. Who would want to be seen with a fat girl? My uncle did arrange for some guy he knew to ask me to the movies once. We went to the drive-in and my uncle followed and parked behind us. The boy sat on his side and I sat on mine until intermission when he got out of the car to get popcorn. When he got back in the car he failed to slide all the way over to his side. He put his arm around me and I started feeling sick. The movie was finally over to my relief, and he slid back under the wheel. He walked me to the door when he took me home and gave me a quick kiss. I made it.....sixteen and kissed, but I was as sick as could be. My stomach churned as the bed cradled my shaking body filled with chills for hours while I lay there hoping sleep would help me escape from this feeling. He never asked me out again, which I was thankful. I decided that this dating thing was not for me yet.

One guy that I was not afraid of was my good friend in school. Art classes brought us together and we were best buddies. I dated him once a couple years after graduation and felt a little more relaxed about boys in general, but turns out he was a homosexual. I never heard from him again, I think he moved out of town.

Like all teenagers I was madly in love. The lucky guy lived in my grandmother's neighborhood. I would plan visits so I could see him as much as I could. He was the most handsome guy I had ever known, and I would have given anything for his affection. My parents knew how I felt about Todd and often warned me about him. They would tell me that he was no good for me, and he probably wasn't, but you can not convince a teenager.

I would go to my grandmother's house and wait for hours to see if he would come to see her, in which he often did. It would thrill me to no end if I got to see him. But my parents had talked to Todd and told him to stay away from me. They told him that I was not his kind. Nothing ever materialized from our friendship and we saw less of each other as we grew older. However, I stayed madly in love with him for several years. Some of my friends were married within a few years after graduation. So my list of people to pal around with became slim.

I worked for a year at a credit bureau right after graduation. I ended up quitting because my boss would not let me have a day off after working there eight months. My Father wanted me to attend business college and insisted that I go. He took me to an establishment that makes student loans and made me get a loan to go to the school. Within a couple weeks I could not get interested and quit school. I had to pay all that money back by myself. My dad was pretty upset but computer key punch was not for me. I wanted to go to cosmetology school, but my dad would not listen to that. Being talented in art and creativity, hairstyling came easy for me. I really wanted to go to an art school in Atlanta, Georgia after graduation but they declined my application since I was overweight. I finally convinced my parents that I wanted to become a hair dresser and started to school in the fall of 1966. After graduating from National Academy of Hair Styling, I continued to stay with the school and teach for a while. I had a real talent for hairdressing and had entered numerous shows.

It only seemed reasonable to me that I should have my own beauty shop. Why should I work for someone else when I could make more money owning my own salon? Besides I was pretty independent and strong headed. I rented a space across the street from the beauty school and my dad put in the walls and we worked hard installing the equipment. *Lady Fair Beauty Salon* opened in the spring of 1968. Two girls were working for me and things were going pretty good, or so I thought. Exposure to the ways of the world had helped me acquire a new set of friends. My new lifestyle and friends disappointed my parents and I couldn't really blame them. By the time I was twenty-one I had moved out with a friend and was taking charge of my own life. Coming and going was my choice now. I was ashamed of my lifestyle, and knew my parents were not at all pleased. They were grieving, but it never changed my choices. Often they would try to entice me to come back home, but I wanted nothing to do with going home or them. I wanted to live my life the way I wanted to. I wanted to have fun.

After about two years I moved into an apartment by myself. Moving back home with my parents was not an option for me although my parents still begged me to come home. It was lonely living all alone, so I started drinking some. I really could not stand the taste so it really never became a big deal or habit with me.

Depression gripped my very soul and I began to lose weight and sleep. Noises invaded my apartment and fear plagued me every night while I waited for the dawn. These were probably the hardest times I had been through thus far. My mother would call every day to check on me when I got home from work. Every weekend my parents encouraged me to come home and go to this new church they were attending. I didn't feel like being around religious people at that time so I came up with excuse after excuse not to go. They were involved in the bus ministry and wanted me to become a part of their outreach. They also sensed my depression and discouragement and reminded me that I could move back home with them at any time. Although I did want to move back home, moving back in with my parents in that tiny little house would be horrible. I was just too proud to do that. However, to keep my parents from nagging me so much I relinquished and attended their church a couple times.

Although, I still had a tremendous fear of men, it never discouraged me from wanting a beautiful life and a happy marriage. Every normal girl dreams of a prince charming and a *"happy every after"* kind of life, and I was no different. I don't suppose I ever wanted anything so bad in all my life..... someone to love me. I just knew this was the answer to my depression and loneliness. Being married would be the total fulfillment and it was my life's goal. Everywhere I went I was on the look-out for Mr. Right. I looked in restaurants, on the street, in the mall, and that is why I started going to church with my parents a little more frequently. I read books and articles on how to be a total woman, how to please a man, how to find the right man and although nothing turned up I was getting prepared. However, the thought did occur to me that I might not ever get married. That depressed me more. All my friends were married and life became pretty miserable as I withdrew into a shell of despair. The only person I had any socialization with was Polly, the girl who worked for me and she had little outside time for me since she was getting married. Not long after she married, she quit working for me so I was having to work many hours to just make ends meet and keep the shop open.

After coming to the conclusion that life really wasn't worth living any longer, I often thought of ending my life. One evening after work I sank deep into my pillow and cried just like I did so often but this time I was so overwhelmed with this misery that I rose from my bed and with determination to end it all, right then and there. I entered the bathroom where I kept my straight razor. "Now was the time, I must end this misery." I could not go on any longer. Life had become unbearable and the loneliness was terrible.

I picked up the razor and looked at the large veins in my arms. I was so much like my dad; I even had large veins like his. I had talked with a girl who had actually cut her wrist several times and she enlightened me on how to accomplish suicide. "Cut your veins lengthwise so you will bleed to death quicker" she said. I would do it. "Now" I told myself out loud and looked up into the mirror so I would not see the blood. When my eyes made contact with the reflection of my eyes in the mirror there was someone else there telling me to "Do it! Do it! Do it now!" Cold chills ran throughout my body. I sensed some presence there with me. Could it have been the devil? I did know that what ever it was, was evil. Not only was I scared to die, but I knew there was a hell and

I knew that I did not want to go there. I was not so sure for the first time in my life where I would go if I died. Actually I never thought about eternity much. The image in the mirror was enough to convince me that I did not want to end my life right then. Being scared out of my wits, I threw the razor down and started crying hysterically. I was terrified of the presence of evil I was feeling. I called my parents although it was after 10:00 p.m. and asked if I could come home to spend the night. I never told them what occurred that night, and I did not go back to that apartment again. I was relieved they ask me to stay. My dad, bless his soul, went back and loaded up all my furniture and things with the help of my brother-in-law.

Life was so mundane with work and nothing waited for me at home except my parents. I would go to my room and sit for hours and watch T.V. A lot of times I would end up going to bed with tears in my eyes. I became desperate and began looking for single meetings. One seemed to be safe so I attended a singles social at a downtown church. To my surprise I met a gentleman and he seemed very interested in me. He asked for my phone number so I gave it to him, but I did not like him and hoped that he would not call. A few days later he called and wanted to come over. It has always been hard for me to say no, so he came over that Friday evening. That same feeling came over me that I had before when I was scared and sick of being around the opposite sex. I made some excuse and never saw him again. What was wrong with me? Was I always going to be like this?

About six months later a friend of mine called and wanted to know how things were going. I had known Kay since we were very young children in church. We would spend the day with each other and play for hours upstairs in her house. We never went to the same school, but kept in close contact through church. We joined the teen choir together and after practice on Wednesday nights we would go get ice cream nearby. Kay married a couple years after we graduated.

She always had interesting tales about her work since she worked in the hospital on third shift. I never knew when to believe her because she either exaggerated or made things up. She told me of a friend of her husband's who she wanted me to meet. Butterflies filled my stomach just talking about meeting him. As I asked question on anything and everything I could think of to ask about him, she assured me that he was a real nice guy and he would not try any funny stuff. We were to meet at Kay's house for supper that Saturday night.

Excitement and fear drove me crazy all week. Finally, that October Saturday night came and I knocked on their mobile home door. My heart fell into my stomach as I stepped inside. At last my fears calmed down as we were introduced. Brad was okay looking, not very handsome, but not ugly. He was about my height and thin. He was twenty-one and I was almost twenty-four years old. It didn't bother me that he was younger but I wondered if it would bother him. That evening went surprisingly well. Time passed quickly and the hours flew by and soon it was time to go. I could hardly wait for Kay to call me the next day with a report of what Brad thought of me. At least he didn't make me sick. Maybe I could get used to him. My heart raced as she told me that Brad was crazy about me and wanted to see me again. I was as thrilled as a silly sixteen year old girl. "Sure", I told her. I liked him too and would like to date him.

Brad called the next day and we began a great relationship. We became good friends and had a lot in common. He was very respectful and quite a gentleman, both sensitive and kind. I was so excited to have someone to care for me at last; it made me feel alive for the first time in my life. As we dated through the holidays, Brad began to express that he was in love with me so we began to talk of marriage for the summer, although I really felt no profound feelings for him. Not to confuse crushes I had on several boys growing up, this felt almost the same way, except this time Brad returned my feelings.

As the New Year approached I had been enjoying meeting Brad's friends and family. His sister was planning a big New Years Eve party and wanted us to attend. I knew there would be drinking there and had not been to that type of party or environment before nor around people who drank. But it sounded like fun so we planned to go. This was the first time I had so much fun during the holidays. Finally, I had someone to share my life with and getting kissed under mistletoe was so romantic.

When Brad picked me up for the party, I was on cloud nine. His eyes sparkled when he saw me and it made me feel confident. I looked great, and felt good about myself for the first time. On the long drive to his sister's house, I began to tell Brad that I had never been around any partying or drinking and for him not to expect me to join in, because " I am suppose to be a Christian and Christians don't do that sort of thing." He seemed to be fine with that although he said very little.

That night was full of mixed emotions. Brad danced and held me close and I felt wanted and needed. Then he danced with someone else and made a pass at her, and I felt rejected and hurt. Later he apologized and said that he should not have embarrassed me since everyone came in couples. It was not long before someone offered me a drink and I took it. I sipped on it and it was horrible but I managed to drink all of it. My head began swimming and I felt woozy but not as woozy as Brad because he passed out. I was feeling guilty because I had not been a good Christian and that my boyfriend was drunk. I had to drive back to my house while he sobered up so he could drive the thirty-five miles back to his house.

Weeks later we began to talk about June being our wedding date, but never got into any details. We knew we had plenty of time for the planning. Brad called and we made our usual date for Friday night, but he failed to show up. Then he stood me up again on Saturday night. I called Kay to see if she knew what was happening and she had not heard from him either. When he stood me up for the third time, I had enough. I knew that he went to night classes at a business college so I showed up there after he got out of class on Monday evening. He sheepishly got into my car and I came right out and asked him what was going on and why did he not show up for our dates. He beat around the bush for a while and admitted that his mother thought I was too old for him. I gave him back his ring and that was the last I saw of him.

Many questions began to flood my mind on the way back home. I did not understand why this was happening to me. I was sure Brad was the one I would spend the rest of my life with. It wasn't like he knocked me off my feet, but I just knew he was the one. That night as I lay in bed crying, I asked God "why?" Again, self pity was my pillow of grief. This had been my one and only chance for marriage, happiness and completeness. I was getting older and there weren't many single nice guys any more.

I talked to God often and kept reminding Him that I was a Christian and that I should not have to suffer the pain of being depressed and alone. Then doubts would invade my confidence and I would begin to wonder if I was really a Christian at all. There began a battle raging within me; then I began to bargain with God. "When I can start living better, God, I will get saved." Another time I would say, "God when I can stop all my bad habits, I will get saved." And again the devil would remind me that "You are okay, remember when you were baptized?" I felt like I was going crazy with trying to decide where I really stood with God. I became confused the more I thought about my eternal destiny and I would try not to think of it.

CHAPTER II

UNVEILING OF THE HEART

ᘓ᛬ᘖ

II Corinthians 5:17 *...if any man be in Christ, he is a new creation: old things are passed away; behold all things are become new.*

Loneliness afforded me many opportunities to talk with God and also give Him every excuse I could think of as to when I could get things right in my life, and get saved; that is, if I was lost. The battle still raging within me was... that sometimes I would convince myself that I was saved, and that my baptism was the proof. After all, I had been to church all my life and had been a good person. Then some nights as I would stand by the window gazing at the stars that sprinkled the sky that still small voice inside me would not let me rest. I became more and more convicted each day that something was wrong with my salvation. Maybe, just maybe I was not really a born again Christian after all. But what did that mean anyway?

The more I thought about my salvation the more I realized that my life had been in vain and there was a void, there was no inner peace. What I needed was a vacation. Perhaps if I went away this gnawing inside me would stop. Things would probably look very different after a change of scenery. Being away would help me realize that I was just imagining all this turmoil within my soul. The devil was probably playing tricks on my mind anyway and trying to make me go crazy. After all I had been under a lot of stress breaking up with my boyfriend. Anyone would be discouraged and imagine things when they go through a hard time like I had been through. But as I reflected on the night that I thought about killing myself, I remembered that I was not secure in my destination if I died. I guess you could say that was evidence enough for me to admit I was lost. No, I still was not sure. Not realizing that the devil was trying to convince me that I was okay put me in a dangerous position. I could have easily trusted what he was telling me.

Now Homestead, Florida was not my ideal place for a vacation, however it was away and I had a high school friend who married a guy in the military and he was stationed there. She had invited me to come down and this was the perfect opportunity. Since I was going, I made plans to meet up with another friend, Pat, who had lived in the same apartment complex as I did when I was roommates with Libby. She and her husband were going to be missionaries and were in Florida to see her parents and make some contacts with some churches for support.

The flight down to Homestead was frightening to say the least. I was afraid of flying and was relieved when we finally touched down. I stayed a couple of days with my friends and then took a flight to Tampa to meet up with Pat. It was a miserable flight. We hit some turbulence which I had no experience with, and I thought we were going to fall right out of the sky. The plane shook violently and I was sure this was the end. I was so nervous my bladder was working overtime. I got up and went to the toilet and as soon as I sat down the "Please return to your seat and buckle your seatbelt" light began to flash. I thought to myself, "This plane is going to crash and they will find me in the bathroom with my pants down." I began begging God for another chance to get things right with Him.

The plane was ascending to get above the air turbulence when I finally came out of the toilet. I was shaking when I sat down so the man sitting beside me tried to calm my fears by telling me that this was normal and it happened all the time over Florida. He began telling me all about the plane and how it was constructed and that we were perfectly safe. I was so thankful I had made arrangements to ride back to North Carolina with Tom and Pat. When we landed I wanted to kiss the ground.

There was something special about Pat. She and Tom were such a sweet loving Christian couple. Right after I moved back home I started attending church more frequently and moved my membership to Parkland Baptist Church. This was also the church my parents attended. Pat and Tom became close friends of mine. They had just made the decision to go to South Africa with Trans World Radio to set up a station that would reach into Europe. Tom had a lot of radio experience and had quit his job to go to the mission field. That week Pat talked about the Lord and how He had supplied their needs. She talked like He was her closest friend. It seemed that she knew Him like she knew her husband. She would add how precious His promises were that she had found in His Word. "Rejoice, and again I say Rejoice" she would quote. She seemed to have something I was missing. She was full of joy and peace even when things went wrong. She did not lose hope when things seemed to come crushing down. Her life was touching me in a profound way and she had something I was lacking and more than that, she had something I wanted. As the old saying goes, "You can lead a horse to water but you can't make him drink," but if you give him enough salt he will want to drink. I was thirsty for that water that only Jesus Christ Himself can give, and Pat made me realize that. She was that salt that made me thirsty for Jesus.

It was March 1972 and time seemed to be standing still. After returning home I had to face the same problem I had left behind. I was sitting in the kitchen talking with my mother about my dilemma of being a helpless looser. It had only been a month since Brad and I broke up and I could not get over the pity party I was having. She listened for a while and I suppose she got tired of my complaining so she turned to me and said, "Jane, you are supposed to be a Christian, why don't you go pray about this! Tell Jesus about your problems."

Those words flew all over me. I was furious. How could she say something insulting like that to me? I became angry and got up and walked out of the kitchen and out the front door. How could I run from this any longer? How could God help me with my problems? I walked down the drive way and turned to go up the street. The cold kissed my tears and I looked up to see the vast darkness sprinkled with flecks of light. My heart melted as I began to talk to God. "Oh Lord!" I cried. "I am so miserable, so terrible, so sinful, you can't possibly want someone like me." My eyes filled with tears blurred my vision of the beautiful full moon, but somehow I sensed God reaching down to me. The still small voice inside my soul spoke gently, "Jane, come. Come to me, don't turn away." "But Lord, there is nothing I have to offer you. I have nothing to give you, there is nothing left of my life." I cried the more. "Come to Me" He gently spoke again. "Lord, I don't know why you want someone like me, but I am yours. Yours to do as you want, for you know I have made a mess of my life, if you can do better, I am yours." His arms engulfed me and as I surrendered my all, which was nothing, I felt his smile of approval.

I came to him with nothing to offer...just as I was! By this time I was at the top of the street. I turned and the tremendous relief of guilt and the weight of all the burdens I was trying to carry were gone. Words could not describe the peace that flowed within my veins. I had stopped crying and gazed toward heaven as I sighed. The moon seemed to be shining in all its glory. I had always seen the moon and stars, but somehow they shown more brilliantly than ever before. Something wonderful had happened and I did not know what it was, but as the weeks unfolded I was a different person for sure. I talked to the pastor and told him what had happened and he wanted me to give my testimony the following Sunday. As I told the congregation of my repentance to follow the Lord, I indicated that I had rededicated my life to Christ. The whole church rejoiced with me as I explained that I had a new purpose in my life, and that was to live for Him.

In the weeks that followed, I realized I had new feelings within I had not felt before. For the first time I wanted to go to church to be with other believers. I wanted to listen to Christian music and to read the scriptures. Wow, something had happen to me and I was no longer the old Jane. I was no longer depressed but determined to give this new experience a chance. I began to spend a lot of time praying, searching, and reading my Bible. Then it finally dawned on me that I had never had a relationship like this before and it was with the Almighty God Himself. I had received the Lord Jesus Christ as my savior and now I belonged to Him.

One evening while watching Billy Graham on one of his Crusade programs I was impressed to write and ask for information for Christian service. The Lord had done so much for me, He had saved my soul, gave me peace that I could not understand and forgave me big time for all the things I had done, why could not I do something for Him? The information was sent and I studied and prayed over the materials and was even more impressed to seek furthering my education in a Christian college. But where, how, when? So many questions, so little answers.

CHAPTER III

IN SEARCH OF GOD'S WILL

James 1:5 *If any of you lack wisdom, let him ask of God, who giveth to all men liberally and upbraided not, and it shall be given to him.*

I was fearful of my dad and it made me hesitant about telling him what my thoughts were about going to Bible College. Twenty-four and still living at home didn't help things either. Dad had helped me a lot by building and remodeling my beauty shop and now I wanted to end that career. Some how I just could not bring myself to disappoint him in this way. Several times I tried but the words just would not come out. One evening he had to run over to my sister's house so I asked to go along so we could talk. Slowly I began to tell him what God had been doing in my life and finally unveiled my plans to sell the shop and go to Piedmont Bible College there in town. I felt like I was disappointing him in telling him this, but it was so heavy on my heart to go back to school. In some ways I knew that he would want me to stay with the beauty shop but I also knew that God was leading me to go to bible college.

"You can't, Jane. You have a business to run." He argued strongly. I could not blame him, he was not a spiritual person, he did not understand.

"Oh yes I can go, daddy. If God wants me to go to college then He will provide a way." Well at least he was informed of my intentions.

I sent for an application in May for the fall semester of 1972 to a Christian college in town. An application came in a few days with a follow-up call from the college. The application and personal testimony did not take long to fill out and I sent it back to the registrar's office. All I had to do now was to wait for an answer. One day I received a call from a very dear sweet lady who said she was the Dean of Women. She invited me to come in and have a personal interview. I graciously accepted and was excited about the prospects of becoming a student. Convincing my dad took some doing but he finally understood that this was what I was going to do. However, he reminded me that the beauty shop was the obstacle. "Who is going to buy a beauty shop?" He asked.

Being a new Christian I did not know what God was capable of doing. Skepticism runs in my family so how did I know that God was even going to answer any of my prayers. But I prayed. "Lord, I am sort of new to all this, and I don't exactly know what to do at this point. I feel that you want me to go to college, but I am not sure. You have got to show me what to do. Lord, I don't know if this is the right thing to do or not but if you really want me to go to school, would you please sell my beauty shop. And Lord, so I will really know for sure it is from you, I am not going to interfere at all. I am not going to advertise or help in any way." Somehow I knew within my heart that God would work things out for me to go. I had been reading in Judges 6:36-40 how Gideon had wanted to know for sure what God wanted him to do. *Gideon said to God, "If you will save Israel by my hand as you have promised— look, I will place a wool fleece on the threshing floor. If there is dew only on the fleece and all the ground is dry, then I will know that you will save Israel by my hand, as you said." And that is what happened. Gideon rose early the next day; he squeezed the fleece and wrung out the dew— a bowlful of water. Then Gideon said to God, "Do not be angry with me. Let me make just one more request. Allow me one more test with the fleece. This time make the fleece dry and the ground covered with dew." That night God did so. Only the fleece was dry; all the ground was covered with dew.* (NIV) For me being a new born Christian, I needed that fleece of assurance. So I put the beauty shop out there for God to sell. I needed a sign.

Later I realize that demanding extra signs were an indication of unbelief and that we have the Word of God that guides us. Gideon just delayed obeying God. If we really study God's Word then we do not need signs to confirm what we already know and that asking for a sign is not a wise way to make a decision.

While working on a customer one day I casually mentioned that I would be quitting work soon to go to Bible College. She had been a great lady who had been coming to me for years. My business had grown and being considered one of the best hairdressers on the street gave me great opportunity to acquire a great clientele. Saddened by my news, she inquired about all the details and how would getting to school transpire and what was I to do with my business. Not being sure myself at that time, she continued, "I know of someone who is looking for a beauty shop to own, are you interested in selling?"

You could have knocked me over with a feather. Could this really be happening? Is this the answer to my prayer? I could hardly wait to tell my dad, but his words were not encouraging nor founded on the faith I was learning about. He responded with,

"Don't count on that. People just talk, and it probably won't materialize. Don't make plans because you don't have any money in your hands."

My response came, "Dear Miss Jane Jestes, We are pleased to inform you that you have been accepted into our Bachelor program at Piedmont Bible College." However, another response came in the form of a check for $2200 that purchased the beauty shop. In two weeks God had sold my shop and I was on my way to college. The money gave me the opportunity to go to school without having to work the first year and my time could be devoted to studies.

The Dean of Women I had met with was such a godly woman. Grace flowed from her like what you would expect out of Jesus. She was kind and gentle, yet exact in her determination. She inspired me to desire to be like her; gentle, meek, glowing, loving and full of the Spirit of God. Godliness oozed from her like I had never seen before or since. She made me feel loved and accepted in a way that I could not imagine. Encouragement was part of her job. I am sure however, a greater concern than a sense of duty was felt by all the girls. So with confidence I stepped out of my car on that first day to register for classes.

There was no one that was recognizable as I approached the building to register. Butterflies filled my stomach. Not realizing that I was not the only stranger there, my self-confidence was at an all time low. Did I wear the right clothes? Are people looking at me? What are they saying about me? Most of the freshmen on campus were about seventeen to eighteen years old. Here at twenty-four years old I just knew that I stood out in the sea of college kids like a big red pimple on a nose. However, I did see one fellow going in at about the same time, who looked as old as me and then I saw a couple of other girls who appeared to be at least my age.

The next day classes began and although preparation had been made, I found myself in a different world. For one thing, I could not understand a thing the teacher of World History was saying. He hypnotized me with his eloquent and intelligent speech so much that I could not even take notes of what he was saying. The man was a genius. Sometimes I noticed that he was thumbing through pages, just to learn later that he was actually reading that fast. It blew my mind away, and I felt like crying because he was talking way above my head.

There was one guy who sat in front of me, with big fuzzy ears, who seemed to be taking notes as fast as the teacher was talking. It was the same guy I saw the day of registration walking across the parking lot.

No one else seemed to be overwhelmed with all of the changes we were having to make or at least I didn't notice that anyone seemed to be having the problems I was having. For one thing, I was not used to Christian language and sometimes I did not know what others were talking about. There were so many things to learn, so much to grow accustomed to doing, so much homework, and getting used to another way of life. Making friends was always hard for me, but one by one a few older students began to socialize in the Student Center. This gave me the opportunity to join in with a group my age. One girl, Levina, and I really hit it off and we became good friends. We had some classes together, and she was an off campus student like me. We would talk of how we became Christians and talk about being single and how it affected us at our age. We were not all that old, but in the seventies, twenty-four was almost an old maid. We both wondered if there were any guys out there somewhere for us.

Several of us would gather in the Student Center and play ping-pong and eat French fries for lunch, especially if we had afternoon classes. Sometimes we would have to hang out for a couple hours between classes. One guy began to hang out with Levina and me and we three would have long talks, like trying to solve the world's problems. He was the guy who sat in front of me in World History with those big fuzzy ears, named Bobby. We would talk for hours even when everybody went home or back to the dorm. I had a good friend like this in high school. You could just talk to him like you had known him all your life. And talk I did. We talked about everything under the pale blue sky.

Out of curiosity I asked him about the rings he had on his fingers. I had been noticing them and was wondering perhaps if he was available. Both were class rings. He had one ring on his pinky; it was a much smaller size. I thought it must be his girlfriend's since it was so much smaller and probably the other was a high school ring. I really didn't know if I was actually all that interested in him, just inquisitive. Since Bobby lived 50 miles away and drove everyday to school, there was no other way to find out anything about him unless I asked. "So, is that your girlfriend's ring?" I asked. "No, actually one is my high school ring and the other is the college I attended, Eastern Carolina." he responded. Well that was out of the way. But did he have a girlfriend? I was afraid to ask.

I never thought about Bobby being a candidate for a future relationship. We continued to talk and play ping-pong through the semester. Then one day he asked me out to go to a Christian singing concert in the next town with him. It was the end of that semester and I thought there would be no harm in going. It had been almost ten months since I broke up with Brad and going out for the evening seemed wonderful. Bobby's parents were there and I met his family. They seemed very nice and were so very proud of their youngest son. But the interest was not there and it did not concern me that he never asked me out again. We were still very close friends and would continue to be. After all, we loved playing ping-pong together and often joked about being Ping-Pong

Pals. We still spent hours talking, but were both contented to be just friends and not to go back out together.

Bob was on the Deans List and made much better grades than most of the class. He was so gentle and kind and would never harm a flea. He tried his best to follow all the strict guidelines of the school. That is why he was shocked when he got a note from the Dean of Men to come into his office for a meeting. What could he have possibly done wrong? Well, later he said that we were reported for spending too much time together. Did that mean we could not hang out together and talk? We did spend all our time together at the Student Center and going to classes together and standing at the cars talking, but that was as far as it went. We both were so hurt by the criticism we thought it best not to talk and carry on like we had been doing. I missed our togetherness, but soon we would break for the long summer and I regained my hope in the plans of serving God in whatever way He wanted.

Summer passed quickly for me since I was canning and helping my parents in the house and garden. I dieted all summer and when the fall semester started I could wear a size fourteen. I was excited about that because that was as small as I had been as an adult. I wasn't quite as enthusiastic going back to college as a sophomore. Classes seemed like a drag. I met up with a real nice guy named Gary. He was especially nice and was married. We became friends immediately and shared a common interest. We both were hairdressers. We began talking about opening a beauty shop business together. We both prayed and God worked. I knew I could not continue school without working some since tuition had increased. Things just fell into place and we asked the Lord to direct us and soon we found a salon for rent in the back of someone's home.

The much oversized lady of the house met us with such kindness, but there was just something about her I did not like. There was something strange about her. Soon after we signed the contract to rent the beauty shop her true identity appeared.

We really did not see much of her but when we did she was drunk. It did not take us long to realize that she was an alcoholic. Sometimes we would not see her for a week. Her neighbors came over to get their hair done and confided in us that she drank most of the time and she could not run her beauty shop anymore. Her husband seemed to stay away from home much of the time.

One day I came to work and she was screaming for help. I went in to her kitchen and there she lay on the floor, drunk and bleeding. She had fell and hit her head and had to be hospitalized for several days. Later it was revealed that this was a regular pattern for her. Not being exposed to such behavior it really terrified me to death. Some times she would come into the beauty shop when she had been drinking and she was mean and hateful. She looked like a madman fixing to kill and I was afraid she would. I asked Gary not to leave me alone in the shop because I was scared of her.

Gary was a unique guy with a loving attitude for everyone. His wife, Pam, did not have a jealous bone in her body, so there were no uncomfortable feelings as Gary and I worked together in the little beauty shop. Many times I would share my feelings with Gary and he became the friend I had in Bobby at one time. Often we talked about the Lord and how he was working in each of our lives and we always pinned up quotes and notes of encouragement for our clientele. We had a lot of students, faculty, faculty wives and church people. Word got around quickly of our talent and atmosphere so we did well financially.

Mid-term exams gave me plenty of time to think about what I was doing, and where I was going. Although I had surrendered to go to the mission field in a chapel service, I had no direct plans. I actually told the Lord that I would go if he would lead and if I did not have to go alone. It was a conviction of convenience you would say. Being alone was not something I had adjusted to easily. Marriage, being a wife and mother and a homemaker was a desire that seemed to be overwhelming. Several times I asked God to take my life if I was not going to get married. I wanted to die by the age of thirty if I was to be single for the rest of my days.

My grades were not all that great and I failed one of my exams. A few times I ran into Bobby in the halls and he seemed to have it all together. I asked him how he made such good grades all the time and he told me the secret. "You just have to know what the professors want." But I never could figure it out. I did not do well in high school either. The Academic Dean was the one I needed to see when I requested to drop school. He tried to persuade me to stay in school since my grades were not the entire reason for quitting.

I felt a firm assurance in my heart that God would have me to continue perhaps at a later time. He could not understand that the peace of God was leading me this way. I told him I would not be coming back to classes. As I was leaving the building in tears, Bobby was coming in.

"Where are you going?" he noticed I was upset. "Home", I said quietly and explained that I would not be seeing him again. He followed me to my car and we talked as he seemed so concerned and sympathetic. "Well, uh, keep in touch, Okay?" he said as I got in my car and drove away. I felt a big relief that I had no more obligations of school.

CHAPTER IV

TELL ME YOU LOVE ME

~:~

Proverbs 3:5-6 *Trust in the Lord with all your heart and lean not unto your own understanding. In all your ways acknowledge Him and he shall direct your paths.*

The next several months were rather uneventful. Christmas came and the New Year went as I lived one day at a time. Gary and I had a great business together and he had also discontinued his schooling. Gary told me that he and Pam were talking of returning to West Virginia. Pam wanted to be closer to their parents, and Gary could get a job back where he used to work.

Robin had become a friend as well as one of my customers. We had graduated from the same high school at the same time but we did not know each other since our class was so large. Robin's and my friendship grew. We would encourage each other and strengthen each other as we poured out our heart's pains. She was concerned that I did not have a boyfriend. Frankly, I did not understand why I didn't except for my shyness. I was rather nice looking, I had been told, so where were all the nice guys? The only answer was that there weren't any left.

One evening Robin called and said she wanted me to meet this young man. A blind date was not my idea of excitement, rather fearful, however I was desperate so I accepted the offer. Robin assured me that I would not be alone with this man, but she and her husband would go along for the ride. It actually helped ease the tension and I had a nice time with him. I called Robin the next day to get the follow-up report. He said he had a good time and that I was a nice girl, but no other comments were offered. I had never met anyone like him before. He was a little older than me, about twenty-nine years old. He had worked for quite a few years and was financially stable. He had inherited his father's business when he suddenly died.

Tim's business like attire impressed me tremendously and I wanted to know more about him. But two weeks passed and I assumed that Tim was not all that impressed with me. One evening he finally called and we set up another time to go out for a date. We saw each other rather steadily for the next three months before I knew where I stood with him.

Tim cried on my shoulders for those months while telling me of his fiancé. They had been engaged for three years and she finally put the pressure on him for a date to be married. He confided that he was so unsure of his love for her and that marriage was such a final step. Not feeling that he could totally commit the rest of his life to someone he was not emphatically sure if he was in love with, he did not obligate himself to a date. She gave him his ring back and found someone else who could make a commitment. Every time we went out, that was all he talked about. I guess he needed a shoulder to cry on and someone to listen, and that is what I became to him.

Somehow I got the impression that he started caring for me and I found myself falling deeply in love with Tim. But there was something that really made me feel uncomfortable. Every time we were out he was commenting on other girls, how attractive they were and looking up and down them. This made me feel insecure with him and although he would tell me that I was pretty, the flattery was not taken sincerely. However, I was happy and in love for the first time in my life and the love bug bit me hard.

The time came when Gary and Pam packed their things and moved to West Virginia. This left me with a tremendous burden trying to manage the shop with all the customers he left behind as well as mine. I was too afraid of the landlady to stay so I rented a booth in another shop but it was a long way out on a main highway. My business fell off because it was so far for the customers to drive. I was disappointed that Gary moved away when our business was going so well, but I had high hopes the wedding bells would be ringing for me soon. Tim began to hint of marriage and it thrilled me as well as my parents. He would say "I am such a poor boy; you wouldn't marry a poor boy like me would you?" My hopes and dreams soared high above the clouds and I anticipated him asking me to marry him at any time. There was just one thing lacking, he had not told me that he loved me. Maybe he found those words difficult to say. Tim was reclusive and did not interject his feelings often.

In June mononucleosis invaded my body and I was in bed for two weeks. The weakness was unbearable and it was difficult to do anything. Tim called often during those weeks and refused to come around since he did not want to contract the horrible ailment. During my recovery he came over a couple times a week after work and I would fix him supper. When I was able to return to work we began our normal routine. On Saturdays he would call about 5:00 or 5:30 to see what time I would be ready and we would go out for supper and a movie. We would end up at my house to talk, have coffee and watch TV. On Sundays he would pick me up after church and we would go to his house for lunch or to his grandmother's once a month in Eden. Often he would come over after work through the week. I would fix supper and we would watch TV.

Tim's mother was a real jewel. She was seeing a gentleman herself and would fix a big meal for all of us. She was a regular customer of mine and she adored me. Often Robin and I would talk on the phone and she knew my excitement and she too was convinced that Tim would ask me to marry him. Although she knew he had not told me that he loved me she was sure that he did by the way he treated me and the things he said. Often he picked and probed me, trying to get me to tell him that I loved him. One evening he kept insisting until I told him, "I love you, now you know." I paused most assured that now he too would confess those words of endearment...I love you too...was what I was waiting to hear. He smiled and his eyes twinkled but instead he said, "Well, I don't love you." I was totally taken aback and embarrassed. The shock on my face revealed my inner pain. Obviously, I had misunderstood this guy. As he explained he said he thought he still loved Kathy, but he was sure he was not in love with me. "Why?" I asked. "Why did you say all those things about marriage, and why did you needle me into telling you that I loved you?" He proceeded to explain that I assumed too much that he really did not mean anything. He was apologetic, but assured me once again that he had no profound feelings for me one bit what so ever. "I think you are an exceptionally nice girl and any man would be lucky to have you for a wife," he added. "But I just don't love you! Now, I don't know if I will fall in love you later and I can't say that will not happen, just give me some time. I really like being with you and spending time with you, but if I want to date someone else I will." "But Tim!" I responded. "I thought we were going steady. You have not dated anyone else and I haven't either these past four months. I see you four nights a week, every opportunity you have and we aren't steady?" His accusing voice declared, "There you go assuming again, Jane".

After Tim left that night I cried a thousand tears, and for the many months that followed. It was not the last time I heard those words ringing in my ears, "Just remember, Jane, I don't love you".

As our dating schedule stayed the same three or four times a week he constantly reminded me that he had no feelings for me. Although I cherished every moment with him, the pain of being reminded followed me to bed each night as I cried myself to sleep. My parents were aware of the anguish Tim was causing me, but said nothing. "But Lord", I would pray, "Why are you allowing this to happen to me?"

Robin became my crutch as we would talk for hours each evening when I was not with Tim. She gave me Bible verses to encourage me and I would hang on to them for assurance. There was one particular verse that became my life's goal and supported me during the days of despair. *"Trust in the Lord with all thy heart and lean not unto thy own understanding. In all thy ways acknowledge Him and He shall direct thy path."* Proverbs 3: 5 & 6. I repeated that verse almost every hour. Trusting the Lord was hard as I would cook delicious meals for him and rub his back. Trusting was, at times, not what I wanted to do, when I made myself available every time he called and sat on the edge of my life waiting for that phone call each day, afraid that he had met someone else.

The rejection took a toll on my mental stability. And I had taken about all I could take. I tried to break off with him, but he kept tricking me, saying "Well, Jane, if you want to take that chance." He always asked if I still loved him, and I did, more and more, but it hurt too much for him to continue to remind me that he did not love me. Several times I would tell him, that I did not want to see him again, but he would call the next day and I would give in. No hope of winning Tim's love finally hit me one Saturday evening. After work,

I rushed home to get ready and waited for him to call just as I had done for the past eight months. I was frantic by 6:00 and angry and enraged by 8:00. He stood me up! I figured out for myself that he must have dated someone else. I even drove by his house to see if his car was there and it was not.

Patience had never been a virtue of mine, and I had run out of patience with Tim. When he did call Sunday morning he acted like nothing had happened, and asked me out for lunch after church. Why would I refuse, I could not stand being away from him. When he picked me up my feelings could not be held back any longer.

"Tim," I pleaded. "Where were you last night? I waited and waited, but you never called."

His response was, "I told you that if I wanted to date someone else, I would."

"But Tim, we have been dating every Saturday night for the past eight months. Why didn't you at least call me to let me know? It really hurt me, you know!"

He was always apologetic and sorry for the way he was treating me, but it also never stopped him. After a long discussion, I told him that I thought it only fair to let me know if he was not going to see me that night. Without saying too much about our relationship which I did not understand, he just kept telling me that he had nothing else better to do. Trusting the Lord in all this became more difficult than I had thought and more than my patience could withstand at times.

Breaking off with Tim became almost a weekly event. He would agree that it was best and that he totally understood only to call back as I waited to hear him say that he could not live without me. Instead, I was reminded that he was not in love with me, but wanted to take me out. I could not resist being with him, and who knows, maybe, just maybe that God was going to give him the love for me I so desperately wanted. Taking a chance on that, I would end up crying each night, but the desire to be with him was greater than my pain.

Robin felt so bad for the way things were going in this relationship, but worse yet, my parents were sick and tired of the way Tim was hurting me. They saw my pain and knew that I cried each time he left. I kept reminding them and myself the same thing he kept telling me, that maybe he would realize one day that he really loved me. "Trust the Lord with all my heart." I was trying. I became lower and lower, and God drew me closer and closer to Himself. No matter how much I prayed I could not see the dawn of this relation-ship. "Perhaps," I told myself, "I wanted too much too fast." But that did not help my frustrations with Tim. I was a young Christian and I would place this whole ordeal in God's hands for him to take care of. I prayed for strength to be patient and to wait for God's timing, but instead I became anxious as I would read Romans 8:28 "All things work together for good, to them who love God." Sure I loved God, but how was this working for my good? What was going on and where was God in all this? I wanted answers.

CHAPTER V

THE GIFT

⌣∶∿

Romans 8:25 *But if we hope for that which we see not, then do we with patience wait for it.*

On October 28th 1974 my alarm clock did not go off. It was Monday and I did not have to work. I sat on the edge of the bed for a long while, praying as I stared out of the window of my bedroom. I had no plans for the day, as usual. I wish it had been raining so I could find an excuse to sleep longer. My dad had just left for work, and I needed to start doing something. Coffee was not my thing in the mornings. Breakfast was no longer a part of my daily routine either since I had lost so much weight. I was so proud of my size now. In total I had lost almost one hundred pounds since I was twenty. Clothes were fun to buy and even shoes fit better. Dressing up for Tim was a delight. He liked the way I looked or he said he did. I really did not know what to believe from him anymore.

While sitting on the bed, I saw a blue car going down the street. We lived on a dead end and I knew every car that came down the street and that car looked only vaguely familiar. It did not belong on our street, but I thought I recognized the guy driving the car. As he came back up the street, I looked again and said to myself, "Is that who I think it is? Can't be." Although the car went past our driveway, I rushed to brush my teeth and comb my hair. I was sure he would turn around and come back as I threw my clothes on. It was only moments when I heard the little blue Fiat rumbling in our driveway. I opened the door and there stood Bobby McCaskill. It was such a delight to see him and remember old times. "Come in Bobby. Gee, it is so good to see you! What brings you by here?"

He said, "Well I had some time between exams and thought I would see if I could remember where you lived. So, how are things?"

We talked for two hours about the people we knew and what had been happening in our lives. It had been a year since I had seen him and he looked better than I had remembered. We talked about what the Lord was doing in our lives now that he was almost finished school. He was finishing in three years instead of four. Bob had taken a lot of extra hours so he could finish school early. Although he did not know what he was going to do after graduation, counseling was a likely path he thought about taking.

Suddenly an idea clicked in my head. I would see if I could get Bobby to ask me out and Tim would be jealous and realize that he did love me after all. When Bobby stood up to leave I said, "Call me sometime and I will fix dinner and we can talk about old times." He said that we would get together again, but I doubted I would even hear from him. He said he was just killing time and he had no outside interest or time except for his studies. I thought to myself, "Here I am again the object of a guy killing time because they have nothing better to do."

During the next week I wondered often if my scheme would work out. I really did not want to use Bobby. He was a real nice guy. But just once wouldn't hurt anyone. I prayed that God would allow Bobby to call and he did. Instead of cooking for him he asked if he could take me out. I did not hesitate one bit. My plan worked and now it was Tim's turn to get stood up and hurt.

November the 9th, promptly at 6:00 p.m. Bobby showed up at my door. It was my twenty-seventh birthday, but I did not let him know. When he came in, we sat around for a few minutes. Tim had not called yet and it was later than his usual Saturday routine call. I was so afraid my plan would backfire and Tim would not call at all and he would not find out that I had another date. This was my whole reason for trapping Bobby into asking me out. We stood up to leave and finally the phone rang. "Oh, I can't tonight, I already have a date. I'll talk to you later, Okay?" I said arrogantly and loved every moment of it. He was extremely curious and I noticed jealousy in his voice as he questioned me. It worked, I said to myself as we made our way out the door.

We had a nice time that evening. He took me out to eat and we both had spaghetti. We laughed and talked just like old times. Afterwards we went back to my house and sat and talked and watch TV. I became drowsy several times and wondered if he had enough sense to go home. I didn't have the courage to ask him to leave, but when he did leave at 4:00 a.m. I was relieved. I was a little concerned if he would be able to stay awake since he had an hours drive back home. Sunday morning I could not wake up for church. I really was not used to staying up like this. I finally got up about 11:00 and took my bath and dressed. I knew Tim would be calling and he did as soon as he got home from church.

Tim picked me up a half hour later for lunch. He wanted to know everything and tried to act like a concerned friend in his interrogation. He wanted to know if I had a good time, and I told him I did. Then he asked if I was trying to make him jealous. I just looked at him and smiled. It was working, my plan was working. All week long Tim kept asking if Bobby called back. And he did, and asked me out again on

Saturday night and I didn't refuse. I thought, a few more dates with Bobby and Tim would be begging me to marry him. But I was feeling a little guilty about using Bobby this way. He was such a great guy and I hated to hurt him. Maybe just one more date would do.

By December Tim was very demanding of my time. Every night he wanted me to be with him. I told him I would not turn Bobby down and would go out with him every time he asked. So every night of the week I was with one or the other. When I was with Bobby, I wanted to be with Tim. When I was with Tim, I felt so bad for Bobby because I was using him.

Tim had quit kissing me in June when I told him that I loved him. He said he could not kiss someone he did not love so he never kissed me again. We did hold hands, and he put his arm around me and he even kissed me on the cheek on occasion. But, all of a sudden he wanted to kiss me again. I was sure that now he would admit that he loved me, but once again he reminded me that was not the case. I was growing tired of rubbing his back while I heard those words ringing in my ears, "Just remember, I don't love you."

Dating every night was a lot of fun but I was getting tired of it too. When I was going to bed at midnight it made getting to work at 8:30 a.m. hard for me. Bobby never left before 4:00 a.m. on Sunday mornings. The merry-go-round that never seemed to stop caused me exhaustion and mixed emotions. I knew I had to choose who I would spend Christmas Eve with and who I would spend Christmas Day with. I had been dating Bobby for seven weeks and did not want to stop dating him. I began to care for him in ways that I did not care for Tim. I respected him because he treated me like I was special.

When it came time to purchase Christmas for the two men in my life, one was a real nice sweater and the other was a bottle of British Sterling. But the decision had to be made who would get the sweater and who the cologne. For some reason the sweater became very significant. It became a symbol of who deserved my love. But the closer it came to Christmas the more confused I was as to who would get it. I had been dating Bobby a little while but he sure showed no feelings at all. He was nice and polite. We were even dating twice a week now, but he never kissed me or held my hand. My parents kept telling me to stop seeing Tim, that Bobby really was the one who cared for me. I told them that I was not sure if Bobby even felt anything for me, because he had not said anything and that I was not going to assume anything any more.

A couple days before Christmas Bobby asked me to go shopping in Greensboro with him and I accepted the invitation. We walked around looked and talked. There were so many things we had in common. We both like Italian food, and shared the same likes in clothes and furniture. We were on our way back to the car when snow began to fall. He took my hand, no words, just a gentle squeeze. Quickly I dismissed any thoughts it might mean something, so I would not assume Bobby had any feelings for me. This was certainly a romantic jester but I did not know if he was serious.

I was so excited about Christmas. I waited to see when Bobby would plan for us to be together before I would tell Tim when I could be with him. I never told Bobby that there was anyone else. I didn't want him to know because I was afraid it would hurt him and scare him away. On the other hand Tim could not stop asking so many questions. "Where did you go? When did he leave? Did he hold your hand? Did he kiss you? When are you going to see him again? Does he love you? What are you going to do about seeing him?" You could say that although I wanted him to be jealous, I wanted more for him to tell me to stop seeing Bobby. However, I was getting disgusted with all his rhetoric and back rubbing.

Mom and dad weren't too enthused that Tim was coming over for Christmas dinner. Dad did not say much but I could tell his feelings by the smoke signals he sent up with his pipe. They were more thrilled that Bobby would send notes all through the week. Every time one would come, my dad made a joke out of it and one day he even taped it to the ceiling and let it hang down in front of my bedroom door. My mother kept telling me that Bobby really liked me a lot, and I would just say, "How should I know. He hasn't told me." But my mom would just reply, "Jane, he is driving fifty miles one way to see you that should tell you something."

The gifts were wrapped, but they lacked names. "Oh Lord" I prayed. "I know these gifts aren't really much at all, but you know the significance that I have placed on who gets the sweater. I just want to make sure I give the right gift to the right guy. Please help me to know who deserves my affection."

By Christmas Eve I was feeling more persuaded to give Bobby the sweater. What could I lose? I was getting no where with Tim. I guess he was really afraid to make any type of commitment. Bobby picked me up early, and we drove the fifty miles to his house. The whole family was there; his two brothers and a sister with their families, and his parents. There were a lot of people to meet for the first time. Everyone was exceptionally nice and made me feel so comfortable around them. Later we returned to my house and I gave him the gift. He opened it and seemed to like it and thanked me for the sweater. He gave me cologne. This time he lingered by the door and talked another half hour. What was wrong with this guy, why doesn't he kiss me? He seems to want to but he acts afraid.

The following weeks were the same with dating every night. New Year's Eve was with Bobby and New Year's Day with Tim. January was cold and it rained almost every day. Every time Bobby picked me up the floor of his car was full of water. We would talk the entire way to Randleman and back. We began to grow very familiar with each other and he would often bring me flowers and send me cards. Bobby seemed so romantic, but still no kiss.

CHAPTER VI

A BROKEN HEART

~:~

Psalms 55: 1-4 *Give ear to my prayer, O God…attend unto me and hear me; I mourn in my complaint….my heart is ever pained within me…..*

When I was not with Bobby then I was with Tim. One Sunday Bobby called and I was with Tim. My mother did not tell him, but just said I was not at home. He was in Winston and wanted to come by. Later he said he thought I was seeing someone else, but didn't ask. He also told me that if I had ever turned him down for a date he probably would not have called me back.

Often my dates with Bobby were spent with the youth group of his church in Randleman, where he was the Youth Director. This week we were taking the youth out to eat so he picked me up early. As we were going down the interstate ramp he leaned over and pulled a white paper out of the glove compartment. He said, "Want to read something I wrote?" "Sure" I said. Bobby was a romantic man who liked to write and read poetry. I opened the paper folded in half and read:

THE DAISY

Music once more dances on the wings of thought. Waves pound the ever shifting sand in marked contrast to gently floating downy clouds. The quiet whisper of a summer breeze caresses the prophetic petals of the daisy as once more I remove the petals in an attempt to try to discover you heart.

I pluck and wait to find if the daisy could tell me whether my love will be returned with love or by some other emotion almost as elusive.

Beneath the summer sky I set and dream with each cloud possessing the illusion of a window in which I may view the past and perhaps catch a fleeting glimpse of the evasive future. In between the glances at my puffy crystal ball another petal comes off and drops to the ground as the eternal question of does she or does she not is again faced with all the uncertainty of a false prophet's message.

Yet, I seem to continue to pluck and wait. The hint of honeysuckle is carried by me on the breeze as if a butterfly were gently brushing a flower.

For a moment I am taken with thoughts of exotic places where the wild flowers are orchids and when the sunset dawns the world is aglow with the shimmering light of myriads of dancing stars. The moon shines brighter still illuminating each languid lapping wave.

Another petal plummets to the now quiet earth. I gaze again at the floating images that fill the sky with millions and millions of stories. Now, as I look up, I place myself in a poetic posture and muse. Tis home that now I think.

The familiarity of those dear essentials that create a home, the smells, the sounds, the work, the play, the love, the discipline, the old, the young, the looks, the smiles and the tears.

Only a few petals more to tell me what I have sought so to know.

I raise my head and look toward the summer sun and behold your silhouette. You touch my hand– the daisy falls– the answer comes, not through petals of a daisy, but through a touch. The touch that whispers ever so gently and ever so true.....I LOVE YOU.

"Well, that was very nice, Bobby. You write very well, expressed so nicely" was all that I could manage. Honestly, I did not know how to react. I wasn't about to make a fool of myself again, and I certainly was not going to assume it had any reference to me. I folded it and put it back into the glove compartment, and made a joke about the water in the floorboard. He had a leak around the windshield and the floor stayed full of water all the time. Then I carried the conversation elsewhere.

One Sunday Tim picked me up after church and took me to his house for lunch. His mother's car had a flat so after we ate he went out to change her tire. I sat on the couch and was looking at the paper when I saw him come out of his bedroom carrying the phone. God gave me great insight with Tim. I knew he had gone into the bedroom to call another girl for a date that night. When he came into the living room he flopped down beside me, he put his arm around me and I said, "What did she say?"

"Huh? What are you talking about?" He asked with a devious smile.

"I said– What did she say? Is she going out with you or not?" My voice trembled with anger.

"Uh, uh, yea" he finally managed.

"You can take me home; I want to go now, Tim." Tears had already blurred my vision.

"Now, Jane....uh....you don't have to feel like this." He said as he stood up with me.

His mother was no where in sight so no apology was needed for leaving so abruptly. By the time I got to the car I was crying uncontrollably. We got into the car and drove the one and a half miles to my house. He begged me not to make him take me home crying like that, he was afraid my father would kill him. Finally I insisted, "Take me home or stop the car and I will walk."

He drove up to the back door and I got out. He said, "Jane, I'll call you later to see how you are". "NO!" I screamed. "Don't ever call me again! And I don't want to ever see you again either. Tim, its one thing to call a girl and ask her out, but to call a girl while you have one sitting on your couch is something else. You have hurt me one time too many, Tim!" I slammed the car door and ran in the house, threw myself on the bed and cried all evening until I fell asleep that night.

Every time the phone rang I would jump to see if it was Tim. And every time it wasn't him. About a month later on a Sunday afternoon the phone rang. I could hear my father on the phone in the kitchen and really didn't pay much attention; figured if it were for me he would have let me know. Then I heard my dad say, "I think you have been told never to call her again, Goodbye" I didn't say anything to him but I could tell it was Tim, and my heart ached to talk to him. I missed him but I refused to be hurt anymore.

I had been praying and God had opened the door for me to be able to move my business closer into town and closer to home. My customers had picked back up and once again my dear dad fixed the beauty shop up for me. I still had a lot of customers from the college and they followed me everywhere I went. My ideal woman, the Dean of Women, was one of my dearest customers. I also kept fixing Tim's mother's hair. She never commented on our relationship except for one time several months later. She wanted to know what happened and I told her. She said she really couldn't blame me for feeling the way I did.

CHAPTER VII

FORSAKING ALL OTHERS

ᴄ⁚ᴠ

Ruth 1:16b ......*For where thou goest, I will go; and where thou lodgest, I will lodge: thy people shall be my people and thy God, my God.*

Bob and I always got along great. After all, we were best friends. I was beginning to think that he really did care for me deeply. One Saturday night we stopped for a snack after taking the youth bowling, and talked for hours. Later at home he put his arm around me and held my hand in his, as we drifted off to sleep. I was so tired and although I enjoyed my time with Bobby, I had wished he would just go home earlier. And here it was again, 3:30 when he finally would get up to leave and then stand at the door for another half hour. We had been dating for over three months and I felt I knew him well enough to know that he was scared to kiss me. After standing there about five minutes, finally I said, "Bobby, why don't you just kiss me and get it over with; you are beginning to scare me". I was beginning to wonder about him. Every time he left I would pray for his safety back home and that he would get the courage to kiss me next time.

"I think I would like that" was his humble reply. It was the sweetest thing I ever experienced. We sat back down on the couch and he put his arm around me and we kissed for about five minutes. I smiled as he left. I should have asked him to do that earlier so he would have left earlier. I said a prayer as usual as he drove away, for the Lord to keep him awake back home.

As usual my mom came bouncing out of bed as soon as she heard the front door shut. It was her routine to inquire if Bobby had kissed me yet. This time I grinned and said, "Yes!" She made a few more comments and went back to bed. It felt so good to lie down in my bed, I was tired. I prayed again for his safety on the road before I drifted off.

Valentine's Day is such a special day for lovers. I didn't know if I fell into that category or not. Bobby had said a few things like, "If you stick around long enough you can watch my hair fall out." But assuming wasn't my game anymore, I had already been burnt once assuming too much. During that week of Valentine's, Bobby sent me another card. This one was a special Valentine's card with a picture of a single rose on the front. The poem inside related everlasting love to a single rose and he actually signed it "Love, Bob" instead of just "Bob" like all the other times. Maybe this was a meaningful sign that he thought of me more than a friend. On Valentine's night he picked me up for our date and brought a single red rose and a box of candy. Later that night he told me that he loved me. This was what I had been waiting to hear but I didn't know if I was ready to return his love so soon after what I been through with Tim.

As the days passed and the weeks rolled by my love for Bob began to blossom into a fragrant example of a lasting relationship. The hours we spent together were sweet and romantic. He wrote me love poems and expressed a feeling that I had never known before, a deep growing love. Someone actually loved me, not for any other reason except for me. I respected that and was proud that such a Godly man chose to love me so much. Much of my past colored my feelings of worthlessness that I felt unworthy of Bobby's devotion and love, but I accepted it with an open heart.

Easter was a unique time of vacation for my family. Since I was a young girl we had always gone to the beach and camped at Easter. My parents belonged to a camping club and every year the club went to Myrtle Beach. Mother and dad had already left for the weekend. My sister and her husband had a camper also, so they left on Thursday with my parents. I was debating whether to go or not and so I asked Bobby if he would like to drive down. He said he had a special Sunday planned with Sun-Rise Services. I had to sing in the choir at my church that morning so we decided it would be fun to go down anyway if only for one night. We didn't leave until after Sunday night services were over and arrived at 2:00 a.m., exhausted. Bob slept in the truck camper with my brother-in-law and dad. No one slept late the next morning. My parents had to leave to go back home. Bob and I spent Monday walking on the beach. We sat on the sand and laughed and talked for hours then rode around until mid afternoon.

While riding around town we drove down a residential section where the houses were really nice. We passed this one house that was gorgeous. He leaned over and said, "I'd like to buy you a house one day just like that."

Now this might seem foolish to say, but I was not going to be presumptuous about anything. All the five hours back home he kept saying things like, "I would like to take care of you." What did that mean? My heart raced but I did not respond.

When we arrived home, Bob was terribly exhausted. He had only about seven hours sleep in three days. We laid down on the floor in the living room and turned the TV on to the music channel. Bob fell asleep and I drifted in and out several times as my mind raced to understand what he had on his mind with all those comments of the day. I let him sleep for a while and when he woke up he looked at me and touched my cheek with his hand. "You know," he said quietly. "There is one thing about you I would like to change."

I chuckled a little and replied, "Well, I knew that you would eventually find something about me you didn't like, what is it?"

"Your last name." he said.

If you are wondering what my response was, I still had those preconceived ideas that I assumed too much. I had no response, just smiled. I kept those thought on my mind and heart as I prayed for direction and understanding. Several days later when I revealed to my mother what Bobby had said she was ecstatic with joy and excitement. Bob had called through the week from the college, but we never discussed the conversation we had on Monday night. When he picked me up on Saturday night we started down the same interstate we had rode so many other times before going to the same place, his home church for a youth meeting.

Bobby was not hasty in making decisions and seemed to weigh every detail in patience and prayer. With my impatient nature, he seemed slow and exact. But I did want to know more about the conversation he started on Monday. "Uh, Bobby, you know when you said you wanted to change my last name? What did you have in mind?" There I finally got it out. "Did you want me to marry you?" I couldn't believe I said that.

He certainly did not hesitate when he answered. "Yea!" he said as he was nodding his head yes. "That's what I meant."

"When?" I asked.

"Soon!" he responded.

"How soon is soon?" I asked.

"Very Soon!" he said.

I smiled big then replied, "Okay, When?"

"After Graduation?" he asked. I said "Okay."

We set the date for our wedding June 28th giving us just six weeks to plan. There was so much to do and so little time. Finally all the arrangements had been made and my big day arrived. As I walked down the isle, I was leaping for joy inside my heart. Tears filled my eyes as I handed a single red rose to my mom and Bob's mom. The ceremony seemed much too short. It was over before I realized what had happened. Such ecstasy flooded my being and I was complete, happy at last. On our honeymoon we decided to go to Gatlinburg, Tennessee, but only stayed there two days. We drove back home, picked up my parents camping trailer and went Myrtle Beach. We had an awesome time riding our bikes, walking and talking. It was so wonderful planning our future together.

Bob found a job working for a group of churches in the downtown area. He was the Director of the Older Adult Ministry at the Downtown Church Center. He was not making much but, we got by in our little one bedroom apartment. He had made application at a school in California to get a Master Degree in counseling. It would be a great future and he would enjoy counseling since he enjoyed helping others with their problems. But until we heard of his acceptance we would continue with what we were doing.

CHAPTER VIII

WHO? ME LORD?

⌣∴∽

Isaiah 6:8 *Also I heard the voice of the Lord saying, Whom shall I send, and who will go for us?*

Bob and I had a great time teaching Junior Church and everyone there was filled with love and warmth. Things were going well until one Sunday evening during the services I noticed Bob's eyes filled with tears. I had never seen Bob cry before and wonder why, while I squeezed his hand to let him know I loved him. He said nothing on the way home and I didn't want to ask why. Later that week he confessed that he wanted to serve God or die. He said life wasn't worth living if he could not serve the One who saved him. I thought we were serving the Lord in our community and church, but he meant something else.

A few weeks later we went out to the same restaurant, Bob took me to on our first date. It was still romantic, just the two of us sitting there talking. After we finished eating, Bob got real serious when he said, "You know Jane, I told you I wanted to serve God. Well, I think He is calling me to be a preacher." At first I thought he was kidding and I replied in a chuckle, "You have got to be kidding, Bobby. You must have it all wrong, because God has never called me to be a preacher's wife." Bob grinned and responded...."Well, I really believe He wants me to preach, Jane." His face was serious. "Okay." I said and we sat there and talked about other things and he did not bring the subject back up.

I continued working as we made plans to purchase a nice little house. We got a good deal on the house since it had been a rent house in need of fixing'-up, but it was in a good neighborhood. It was exciting to see God answer our prayers in every detail needed to purchase the property. Within three months after our wedding, we were in our own home. It was a three bedroom and two bath house with a large den, living room and a kitchen. My dream home with a large yard had become a reality. It was hard to believe that God had blessed us so much. We had a lot to do to the house to fix it up the way we wanted it and it was hard work. We painted and antiqued paneling, put down carpet, and transformed the place. We did all we could do with the money we had.

One morning after Bob had left for work, I was reading my devotions and the scripture was Romans 8:28. "I beseech you therefore, brethren by the mercies of God, that you present your bodies a living sacrifice, holy, acceptable unto God which is your reasonable service." There in the space after the word "service" was the word "YES". God reminded me that I had written that word "Yes" in a chapel service in 1972-73 school year while I was in Piedmont. A guest speaker had impressed me during his sermon, to give my life to the Lord and his service. He said that God wanted a living sacrifice not a dead one. Then he challenged every one of us to answer that question: "Would you present yourself to God as a living sacrifice for His service? If so, then put 'yes' right in the margin." It made me a little uncomfortable for the moment, why would I say no. I stared at the "YES" for a long time. Tears filled my eyes as I felt God tugging on my heart. "What does this mean?" I thought. I kept those thoughts to myself for the next several weeks and kept asking

God what I must do. Did He want me to be a missionary? Somehow I felt that He did. What about Bob? What would he say and how could I convey this to him? The Lord gave me a peace that I could not understand and the ability to trust Him in all that was occurring in my thoughts. My prayer was for God to speak somehow to Bob if he wanted us to be missionaries.

It was a cool evening in October as we drove my dad's truck back from his parents' house. They had given us a picnic table for our backyard. We were thrilled to have the table but my heart was heavy with needing to talk to Bob about being a missionary. About half way home we started talking about how the Lord had been working in our lives. And I asked, "Bob, does serving Him mean that you would go anywhere in the world the Lord wanted you to go?" He said, "Yes, I would, Jane." With excitement in my voice I said, "You mean that? You would even go to another country?" His response thrilled me, "Yes, I think I would, Jane. If I knew in my heart that God wanted me to go I would." As we talked we began to discover that God had been working in both our hearts at the same time. We both felt that He was leading us to become missionaries.

Bob and I were ready to pack our bags and leave the country without another thought. However, we talked it over and thought that we needed to meet with our pastor. He would be excited too to hear of our decision. For several days that was all we could talk about. Then when we sat down with our pastor he began to ask question that we had not thought about. Where were we going, what country? What mission board are you going to be affiliated with? How long will it take you to raise your support and how much do you need to raise? We didn't know there was so much to think about. When we left we realized that this took some time and thought and most of all, prayer. We were still excited but a little overwhelmed with all the details.

November 9 my parents had us over for supper since it was my birthday. They gave me some things for the house and I began to cry. They could not understand, but for me, my heart began to break as I realized that I would have to give up the very home the Lord had blessed me with. I had been waiting for years to finally have a marriage, a husband and a home. Now the Lord was asking me to give it back. We had only been there three months and I was crushed. This was a lot the Lord was asking, but I did want to do His will and I did want to serve Him. I knew there would be sacrifices to make but I was not prepared for how much it would hurt or cost. We could not turn back, we could not resist His will as we were drawn to his precious love and He comforted me and sustained me though the sacrifices I had to make. He had sacrificed so much for me. My house was nothing compared to what He went through to purchase my redemption.

One of the first people we wanted to share our plans to be missionaries were the Delnays. Dr. Delnay taught at Piedmont and Ms. Delnay had been the Dean of Women. We invited them over for supper one evening. They were always such super people. She brought me a candle when they came. We shared with them how God had been working in our lives and they were so encouraging. They seemed so excited to know that we would be serving the Lord.

I remember when we told my parents about our plans to become missionaries. My Mother cried and said she would have cried harder at the wedding if she knew Bob was going to be taking me so far away. We had a very close relationship, my parents and me. They had married when mother was sixteen years old and dad was twenty-one. I was born nine months and two days later. Mom was so young, it was actually like we were sisters and some times people kidded us about our ages. She said she had always prayed that God would use me in some way, but she had no idea He would send me away. Dad did not say much as usual, just puffed on his pipe like he did the night Bob asked him if he could marry me. When we told Bob's parents one evening in our living room they just sat there on the couch in dead silence. For a little we looked at each other wondering if they even heard us. There just was not any response at all even when they left to go home. We were puzzled as to what they must be thinking. It took several weeks for them to make any response at all. It hit them harder than we had imagined.

The first assignment was to find a mission board. We did not have any idea where we wanted to go yet, but we knew we would need help in getting there. We contacted a board in Chattanooga, Tennessee that welcomed us with a packet of information on how to apply to their mission board. As we spoke on the phone we were informed to get our papers filled out immediately so we could be processed for the January meeting. Within weeks we were notified that we would be set up for a screening and then the final vote would take place while we were in town to inform us if we would be missionary appointees for their organization. They had no problem in us not knowing where we wanted to go yet. They said that could be settled at a later date.

January came quickly and we drove the six hour trip to Chattanooga directly over the mountains. We wanted to arrive the day before our appointment so we could be well prepared for the interviews. We checked into a modest hotel and anxiously waited for the next day.

We had coffee before we drove into town for our meeting. This day made us more nervous than our wedding. As we were met by the president of the board and his wife at their home, we knew this was God's path for us to take. Although they were very gracious, we were still tense. There were five men that interviewed each of us separately and then together, and then dismissed us while they voted on our acceptance with the board. The wait seemed endless, but they summoned us with smiles as they gave us a congratulation handshake. We felt so relieved that was over as we climbed into our car and headed home. But as we were driving the long way home we discovered that we did not know what to do next. They just said goodbye and that was that. We were so full of questions. We needed to know step by step how to raise support and what we needed to do next. When we arrived home we called and began questioning them about all that Bob and I had talked about on the way home. They must have been amused at our ignorance, but it was all Greek to us. We were now officially Missionary Appointees and on deputation. This is when missionaries go from church to church and present what they will be doing on the mission field. The churches will hopefully discuss supporting you. Then you wait and pray that God will lay it on their hearts to support your ministry.

We knew we wanted to serve the Lord on the mission field somewhere and we needed to know where the Lord wanted us to go. We got the map down and looked at the world. It seemed that a lot of missionaries were headed to Africa, the Philippines, Brazil and other South America areas. No one we knew of was going to Europe.

There were a lot of documentary films on the TV that Christmas about Italy and that seemed to hit us hard. We began to ask the Lord if Italy was where we needed to go. One day I asked one of my customers that traveled a lot what was the most interesting country and she said, "Italy, no doubt". I mentioned it to Bob and he seemed interested and we began some research on the country and their religious beliefs although we knew it was predominately catholic. After we prayed and studied all the countries we pinned down Italy and God gave us amazing peace about going there.

There was much to learn about Italy. Some things we found out about their religion by watching the documentaries. They believe that the Pope is God's representative here on earth. They believe that Mary is mediatrix with Christ.

You are encouraged to pray to statues and saints. They teach that salvation is in the Catholic Church alone and that you are saved at infant baptism. You must be confirmed into the church at twelve years old and do everything the priest tells you. When you die you go to a place called purgatory and wait for some priest to pray you out. Of course all this costs money. We were so saddened to think that the people in Italy were not told the truth of God's Word. There was so much more we would learn in Italy.

When we realized that deputation might take us a long time, we prayed about starting our family. I had been to the doctor for hormone problems since I was a teenager and made an appointment with the endocrinologist to find out what could be done. After some tests they suggested adoption and said that I did not produce the right hormone for ovulation and it would be doubtful that I could get pregnant. My chances of conception were less than fifty percent. They would start the paper work for adoption at my word. Bob and I weren't sure how much that would cost or if we even wanted to discuss that at length.

One day I was running into the house and tripped through the back door and fell. Fortunately I caught myself, but I landed on my arm and jammed my shoulder badly. I was in a lot of pain and my mother suggested that I go to the chiropractor to see what he could do. With jamming my shoulder I also injured my back to the point it was affecting my nerves. It took a long time for my shoulder to mend, but he told me that my back was causing my hormone problem and that he could adjust my back where I could have children. All right, I thought. I believed that God could do more than I could ask or think, abundantly so. I guess he could use the chiropractor if he wanted to do that.

We had put our house on the market in June although we were told it was a bad time to be selling a house. Meanwhile, Bob and I worked on getting a display and a slide presentation together so we could start visiting some churches. We did not know what to expect out of deputation, although we had heard some other missionaries commenting on their experience. It didn't sound all that bad but it took sometimes a couple of years to raise support, depending on where you went and how much money you needed. Our board had given us some idea of how to go about raising the support, but we were pretty much on our own.

CHAPTER IX

UNBELIEVABLE ACTS OF GOD

﹏:﹏

Hebrews 11:6 *But without faith it is impossible to please him; for he that cometh to God must believe that he is and that he is a rewarder of them that diligently seek him.*

There was an American church in Italy that contacted our board and wanted to know if any missionaries were coming their way that they had some nationals that needed a pastor and wanted to start a church for the Italians. The thought of that sounded great, and we contacted them for some additional information concerning Italy. They told us that we would need about nine hundred dollars support each month. Now we had an idea and a goal that we could share with our churches. Nine Hundred Dollars a month sounded like a lot of money to us. Bob was only making about five hundred dollars a month at that time and we were making our bills. We knew also that we would need what is called passage and outfitting. That is your air fare and shipping all that you need to take with you. So after we collected the information we put everything down on paper in letter form so it could be part of our presentation for the pastors because they always asked what was needed and what we had.

Bob had called several pastors and finally got a meeting in South Carolina. He got off work early that Wednesday because the drive was four hours. We needed to get there early to set up our projector and slides, meet the pastor, get the tape recorder keyed, and be ready by 7:00 p.m. to start. Some of the people of the church met us with complaints about the pastor and some things that were expected by them. One hostess said the pastor got all upset with her because she wasn't at church Sunday morning because she was sick. She had to sing in a wedding that afternoon and the pastor reprimanded her harshly because she was too sick to attend church but not the wedding. This was very strange that these people were telling complete strangers like us about their pastor. We presented our work and questions from the congregation were asked. The pastor asked to see Bob after church services. After we loaded our things into the car he proceeded to set us straight, saying that Bob was an ungodly man with his mustache and that my dress was too short and too low cut. I think I cried all the way home. It was not an impressive first experience for what was supposed to be our ministry for the next couple years. Our mission board called us the following day and said the pastor had called him and was complaining about us. He said not to worry that the guy was strange and for us not to be upset about it.

We did not realize that we were embarking on new territory that we knew nothing about. We were young and impressionable didn't know what to expect from churches or pastors. Very little did we know about deputation or what to expect. God had some important things for us to learn and some great experiences that we would never forget. There were missionaries that we would meet that would enlighten us on the good and bad things of being on deputation. We would make new friends, learn about ordinary people in ordinary places, be hosted by the poor and needy them-selves, have our hearts melted, find ourselves in strange and awkward circumstances, challenged by the problems, accept the inevitable, and know more about the God of all grace and mercy. And we also learned that we were just like everybody else. There was nothing special about us. But we began to feel like we were on display for any body to criticize. If the people liked you, liked your presentation, if you had a great voice and could sing, liked your preaching, then you might have a chance of getting sometimes twenty-five dollars a month support, or maybe even fifty dollars.

Deputation was not a great way to raise the support a missionary needed. Often times not only us, but we heard most missionaries complaining about the miles they had to travel, the cost of a three year term just to get the support, the stress on the family, and the treatment received by pastors. Mission boards were also a sore spot among missionaries. A large percentage of missionaries who start out on deputation never make it to the field because of the problems of raising the support, the discouragement, and the stress. We adopted a philosophy that it would be much better if churches would support fewer missionaries for larger amounts. (I guess there would be no glory in that. It would look better to support 500 missionaries for $5 than to support 5 for $500.) That way it would not take as long for them to get to the mission field, it would not drain the budget of the missionary and be less stress on their families. It also would not take as long to visit the supporting churches and report back to them. By the church having more invested it would also give them a greater responsibility to partner with the missionary to accomplish specific goals on the mission field.

Well, we had a few more meetings during the summer as Bob tried to work then turn around and try to travel on the weekends and Wednesdays. Sometimes we would not get home until 2:00 or 3:00 a.m. We tried to limit our traveling until August. We were informed of a big mission's conference in Stone Mountain, Georgia and that they would probably be adding new missionaries for support. We were told that it would be good if we could go, but we had no money for traveling. We prayed and asked God for some extra money to go to Georgia and to our surprise God sent it. A few days before we should leave the money came in the mail in the form of a refund check. We should not have been surprised, but we were so new at asking God for something we really needed. *"But my God shall supply all your needs."* the missionary Paul wrote to the church at Philippi. And we were going to learn that God would supply all our needs. All we needed was to ask and then trust God. But this lesson was to be reaped many times before it ever sunk in, that God could do more than we could ask or even think.

Luke 1:37 *For with God nothing shall be impossible*

The Stone Mountain Missions Conference changed our lives forever. When we first arrived we were met by the host of the church. We introduced ourselves and told them what board we were with and said that we had been told that there would be accommodations for us. They told us all we needed to know about the conference times and places to be and escorted us to our quarters in another part of the church. Men were on one side of the hall and the ladies on the other side. Cots were lined up against the wall where they had turned classrooms into make-shift dorm rooms. I did not like the arrangement of being separated from Bob one bit. This was the first time we had been apart since we were married and it was an uncomfortable setting. But God was not interested in my comfort right then. He had greater lessons for me to learn than listening to my complaints. There were a few other women and children around. Some were so shabbily dressed they could have been mistaken for homeless people.

Some others came with camping trailers so they could have their privacy.

The meetings began on Monday afternoon and the following day we met at 9:00 a.m. We had never been to a mission's conference before and did not know what actually happened at them. There were testimonies of God's blessings, preaching for a while, singing, and more testimonies. Bob stood up and said he had a testimony of how God had supplied the money we needed to come to this great conference. Truly God was blessing our hearts in all that we had seen and heard. A short time later an offering was taken, but we had only some change to drop into the plate as it passed. The pastor of the church said to the ushers, "See that couple over there," pointing to us, "Take them all the money, don't even count it, just give the offering to them." We were astonished and a little embarrassed too. There was about seventy dollars in the offering, just what we needed for the trip back home. We felt that we were obeying God by going to this conference and actually had not thought about how were going to get back home until God had supplied us with the money. God provided for the entire trip.

That whole week was such a blessing and inspiration to our souls. God lifted our broken spirits and we began to see a new light of what excitement and joy it was to see God at work in our lives. We had gotten a taste of what God meant by "faith as little as a grain of mustard seed" and our hearts were blessed. There was another speaker at the conference who was a pastor of a church in North Carolina. He was a missionary appointee to Chad, Africa. He also was there to raise his support, but was also the guest speaker. He was quite a dynamic speaker and I really enjoyed listening to him. His topic that day was "Faith." It was so ironic that the more we were learning about faith the more we realized we knew little about it.

He told of a couple in his church that had wanted children and had been married for several years, but could not conceive. (Sounded like me.) They had come to Jack and asked for advice, and he told them that God would answer their prayer and they would have a child if only they would have **Faith**. He told them to pray without ceasing, to pray morning, noon and night for a child, and they did. A year later they were holding their new born son that God had given them. For the first time we were beginning to comprehend a little about **Faith**. It is the ability to **Trust** God for anything and everything. "Trust," seemed like a small word. So I looked it up.....confidence or faith in a person....to believe in......to expect.......to depend on. We had touched only the tip of the iceberg when it came to learning about this thing called "Faith". *Faith sees the invisible, believes the incredible and receives the impossible.* (Author unknown) Sure we had faith in God to save us. That is a real leap of faith. But this was something altogether different.

The week we arrived home from the conference we were on top of the mountain. We decided to pray earnestly every day, three times a day, for God to give us a child. We knew we could trust God just as anyone else could. One day Bob called home from work and said, "Jane, you know ...I have really been thinking about that message on faith." "Yeah? I have been a lot too." I answered. "Well...." he was hesitant, "I just think we need to trust God more if we are going to get to the mission field." My response was, "What are you talking about Bobby?" He quickly answered, "I don't know, I'll talk to you when I get home this evening." I was afraid of what I was thinking, and when he came home and told me what he had in mind I was getting really scared to think what lay ahead. Bob was talking about going on deputation full time, trusting God completely to provide. I thought we were trusting God completely. That meant he would quit his job and we would travel all the time from church to church, city to city, week in, week out. What would others say? What would everyone think? Where would the money come from? Well, Bob did not know either, but he was sure this is what God wanted us to do. I was not so sure, but we talked and prayed about it and all the other missionaries seemed to be doing okay on full time deputation, raising their support. Bob gave a thirty day notice at work as we felt God directing us in this way. One month's salary left what then?

I was shocked when I opened the mail and I had a six hundred and fifty dollar bill from the IRS. They said I owed taxes for the last quarter in 1975. I contacted my book-keeper I used for the beauty shop and sure enough he had forgotten to tell me I had to pay an estimated tax for that last quarter I worked. That was another financial burden we had not expected outside our house payment. I went to the IRS department to make arrangements to make payments and the woman was so nasty and down right indignant. I left feeling humiliated and most of all embarrassed. She made me feel like human trash. I knew I had to get her off my back somehow. It was an honest mistake; I was not trying to get out of paying what I owed. We did not have six hundred and fifty dollars to pay all at one time.

Our plan was to have a yard sale and see what we could come up with. We had to get rid of the stuff we didn't need anyway since we would be leaving the country. My parents donated stuff out of their attic (most of it mine) they had accumulated over the years. One Saturday in September we had our entire front yard full of junk. I wasn't feeling my best that day. I felt sort of strange and kind of sick at the same time. I had not slept much or well the night before so I was tired.

Almost everything sold, old tires, carpet, aquariums, an old sewing machine, anything we could get our hands on we sold. It was unbelievable. We had only one small box of stuff left. We totaled up the sales and we had about $680. We had enough to pay the IRS and some left over!

Bob and I made a commitment to always pay our bills and tithe. If we had anything left over we would eat and we always ate. It was our responsibility as a Christian to pay our debts; our testimony was on the line. God has always honored that in our lives. We knew of too many Christians who had a poor testimony when it came to paying their bills and we didn't want the lost world point their finger at us and say something bad about us being a Christian. We wanted to guard ourselves and not mess up for the cause of Christ. God has always made that possible.

We had been asking the Lord to sell our house. It had been a year now since God had first worked in our hearts and we knew we wanted to be missionaries. This year had gone by so quickly and there was still so much to do. Bob's job was coming to a close and we were preparing to move in with my parents so we could save money. We were receiving fifty dollars a month support but that did not go very far. We prayed and God worked all the details out about our house being sold. Once again He showed us that we could rely on His timing and His plan. As we were making final arrangements to move out of our house and into my parents' house I was filled with mixed emotions. I had reason to be sad because I was losing my home, and moving back in with my parents. We had no home, no income, and no money. All I had was questions. It was a very insecure time for me. I did not know what was expected out of our new position as missionaries. Did that mean we could never have anything else again? I remembered how cruel people were when we would visit their churches. One fellow said to me, "I could be a missionary....I ain't proud......I could beg too." That made me feel like we were beggars. We were going from church to church visiting other Christians and some of them made us feel cheap and degraded. I thought this must be how it was, and we accepted our role and humbled ourselves to take what ever we could swallow without complaining just so we could get the money needed to go to Italy. It was also amazing how now all of a sudden our friends drifted away.

The day we moved into my parents' home, I found out that I was pregnant. It was a joyous time for Bob and me. Once again, God proved himself to be faithful. We could not praise him enough for answering our prayers. We knew now that we could not stay long with my parents; there was no room for a baby bed.

We were uncomfortable at my folk's home, needless to say. We knew there were whispers because we had moved in with my parents. It appeared to others that we were lazy and Bob would not work or hold down a job and we were mooching off my parents. Had we misunderstood God's direction? Bob quitting his job for us to go on full time deputation was a huge leap of faith. Where was God in all this? We were full of questions as Bob tried to make contact with pastor after pastor for meetings. I had been sick and then I got the flu and did not want Bob to leave at times. My parents did not understand and it was way too hard to explain. Did not God say in Luke 14:26 and verse thirty-three what the cost was to be a disciple, to follow Him? We were forsaking all; we just did not know that our own families would be our worse critics. We thought our families would always be there to support us, but we knew that when Jesus himself testified that a prophet had no honor in his own country, that held true for us as well. (John 4:44) It was our cross to bear, to be dishonored by our own.

In February we went to Florida and stayed with Bob's brother so we could try to make contacts in Tampa. While we were there one Sunday we visited a little church close to their home. They found out we were missionaries and gave us a blanket they had been making by hand. They were so proud of it and said they had been praying to be able to give it to a missionary but did not know of one anywhere. People like that blessed our hearts and gave us encouragement that there were Christians who did care and pray for missionaries.

Our greatest concern when we returned was to move out of my parents' home. Our home church had a fifty by ten foot trailer behind the church property. In March they offered for us to use it to live in. We now had one hundred and fifty dollars a month support and thought we might have enough to pay the electricity bill and doctor.

We could hardly wait to move to our own little place. Words alone could not express the gratitude we had in our hearts to our church in providing us a place to live. The trailer had two tiny bedrooms, a kitchen and living room and one bath. It was very small but it was a place to call home. We had purchased a couch we saw advertised in the paper that had a bed; just in case we needed extra space for company. When we brought it home we could not get it through the door. Bob and the preacher had to remove the window to get the couch in and we left it there when we left it.

There were many things we needed for our baby. I had made curtains from a print of Raggedy Ann and Andy and a blanket to match. I had my eye on one particular baby bed, but did not know how we were going to be able to afford one hundred and sixty dollars for it. I did find out that if we drove to Basset, Virginia we could get it for about one hundred dollars. I told my mother about the bed in excitement but she was quick to reply, "Jane, don't forget you are missionaries now, and missionaries don't have nice things like that." Was this true? Were we that different from anyone else? I was still hurt over having to give up my house, and now I felt guilty for wanting nice things and thought maybe I shouldn't be so materialistic and selfish. However, God supplied the one hundred dollars necessary to get the bed as well as twenty dollars for gas and we drove to Virginia to get the bed.

Bob and I were getting a glimpse of what some folks thought about missionaries. Not only my parents but others as well asked us all kinds of strange questions and made off the wall remarks which indicated not only their ignorance but their idea of what a missionary was. We were not orphans, we were not homeless, we were not beggars, we were proud, and proud to be ambassadors for Christ. We considered it an honor to serve Him, regardless what others thought. Sometimes family members made ugly remarks and we would get our feelings hurt. Their view was that we were just lazy failures. Often we were humiliated by so many put downs and hurt by lack of support but Bob would not lose sight of his goal to serve God. We found out that the cost of serving God was not popular. Maybe we made folks feel uncomfortable around us.

My father especially had a hard time accepting Bob because he had always worked so hard to provide for his family. He was a manual laborer and it was hard for him to understand anyone who would want to read and study God's word and live by faith. Bob and my father were complete opposites and my father could not handle it. The friction was difficult for me to handle at times. I felt like we were letting our parents down and that they had a hard time accepting what we were doing. Sometimes comments were being made because we did not compare to our siblings successes and we did not know what the future was, but we knew the One who held it for us and trusted that he would guide us through this path.

Being pregnant wasn't so bad, but the waiting for the due date was wearing away at my patience. My due date had been set for May 5th which conveniently came and went. I was getting more miserable by the day. They changed the due date again, and again it came and went. About June 7th the doctors said I was overdue and decided to induce labor but that did not work either so they said I must not be due yet. I was in tears because I was afraid they were going to let the baby die. I knew that I had been pregnant at the yard sale in September so that put me a month overdue. The next week when I went to the doctor they came to the conclusion that they knew I was pregnant when I came in, so I had to be due and more than likely, overdue.

They could tell the age of the baby by the amniotic fluid so they did an amniocentesis. They drew blood instead. The doctor did another one, and got the same results. They transported me to the hospital to do another one, this time while doing a sonogram. By looking at the image of the child they could make sure as not to insert the needle into her, but this also gave them nothing but blood. The doctor became puzzled and seemed quite concerned and said he did not want to do anything else since he must be hitting the placenta. He stepped out of the room to talk with the other doctors. When he came back he said there was nothing left to do except a C-section the following morning.

The next morning our daughter, Amanda Lynn was born at 10:20 a.m. weighing seven pounds and six ounces. She seemed to be fine except for the trauma of being a month overdue. Bob and I were so proud of her and when I came out of recovery we got to hold her for the first time. As we gazed into each others eyes a special oneness bonded us like nothing else before this little life we were holding came into our lives. She was a part of each of us, and we were overwhelmed that God had created such a beautiful thing. He was truly amazing and awesome to create us the way he did. I counted each of her toes to make sure she had all of them and checked her over like all new mothers do. She lost weight at first which was normal and was very skinny from being over due. Everywhere she had a wrinkle her little skin was cracked from drying out in the womb.

I took her home in the same dress I wore home from the hospital twenty-nine years earlier. My grandmother had handmade a little white dress and petticoat to go underneath. When I was sixteen years old my grandmother took it out of an old chest and said she had been saving it for me. The dress was not very pretty nor well made but I was so proud of it and was excited to get home and show Amanda off.

CHAPTER X

A JERK IN THE CHURCH
~:~

James 1:2 - 3 ...count it all joy when ye fall into various trials, knowing that the testing of your faith works patience.

Amanda was three months old when I resumed traveling with Bob on deputation. We borrowed my parents' trailer often so I could go along if we had to stay over night. More times than I can remember we had no money to get us from one place to the next. We lived at the hand of God, literally. Someone at a church would come up and hand Bob five dollars not knowing that was our next meal or gas to get us home. We saw how He supplied, and it amazed us at how God would never let us down. We always had enough, nothing left over. Often we thought about the children of Israel when God provided manna from heaven each day with nothing left over. He was teaching them to rely on his provisions, just like He was also teaching us.

Our support level rose, but also did our financial responsibilities. We now had about three hundred dollars a month support, but there were ear infections and regular doctor visits. Many times we did not have any groceries and we would not let anyone know about it. On occasion someone would come by and bring us something out of their garden and often my mom would bring leftovers that my dad was not fond of. We were so thankful to get them. I remember one time that we had no money and nothing in the house to eat. A friend of ours in the church had lost his job and they too had a baby about the same age as Amanda. The church took up and had a food drive for them. They had received so much they could not use it all and brought three bags of food over and asked if we could use them because they had too much. We sure could use them and learned that God continually supplied our needs and we did not have to tell anyone about them. Bob and I felt that we did not need to share our situation with anyone, but just waited to see how God was going to supply and He did. But Bob and I were the type of people who could not ask.

It was so well put in *Our Daily Bread,* November 30, 1985

If we could look behind the unexpected events in our lives, we would be amazed to see God wonderfully providing for our needs. The insignificant turns in the road, the seemingly unimportant events, the often unexplained happenings, all are part of God's loving care.

His gracious providence is also evident in the tangible provisions of life. In Bristol, England, George Muller operated an orphanage for two thousand children. One evening he became aware that there would be no breakfast for them the next morning. Mueller called his workers together and explained the situation. Two or three prayed. "Now that is sufficient," he said. "Let us rise and praise God for prayer answered!" The next morning they could not push open the great front door. So they went out the back door and around the building to see what was keeping it shut. Stacked up against the front door were boxes filled with food. One of the workers later remarked, "We know who sent the baskets, but we do not know who brought them." -P.R.V

We were learning that God never wastes anything. He was using these valuable experiences to grow our faith in Him alone. We were also learning to be patient and to wait. That seemed to be so much a part of this deputation thing. Money was certainly slow coming in. At times it seemed that God was silent. Everything seemed to be on hold.

In the spring of 1978 Bob was away on a five day trip to a mission's conference. I got very dizzy and went to my parents to stay so they could help me with Mandy. The doctor checked me out and said everything was fine but it must be that I was not eating properly since I was nursing. The dizziness lasted for about three days then went away. This was just the first episode of what would color the next twenty years of my life.

Two months after Mandy turned one, I was pregnant again. The Lord sure was blessing me since the doctor said I probably could not have children. I knew that this would mean another C-section and my travel this time would be even more limited with two children, but I was determined to be with Bob as much as possible and continued to travel with him every chance I got. We enjoyed being together, and we could not stand the thought of being separated for any length of time.

Our mission board contacted us and told us to be at a mission's conference in Pensacola, Florida in August at a church that supported us for ten dollars a month. We were told to be there Monday that Bob would be speaking Monday night. Bob told him that we could not make it by Monday that we already had a meeting set up for Sunday night in West Virginia and there was no way we could drive and be there on Monday. He told them we might could make it by Tuesday and that he could speak then. I had gone with Bob to West Virginia so we had drove half the night to get back home. We were so exhausted we slept until 9:00 a.m. but managed to get away and drive half way Monday night. The car was doing terrible and drinking gas like crazy. We had no choice but to use the credit card. The following day we left early and stopped only for gas, which seemed often. We finally arrived at the church, pulled up in the parking lot and the car literally died. Several men came out and they managed to push the trailer around so we could hook up where we needed to be.

The pastor and our missions' director came out and were angry and upset. It seems that there was a grave misunderstanding and they were expecting Bob to speak on Monday night. Bob said "I told you I could not get here by Monday; I had a meeting Sunday night". But they were not going to let that slide by. They did not let Bob speak at all since they said he was supposed to be there Monday night and speak. The pastor also did not acknowledge that I had a name and call me Mrs. Bob. I told him several times my name was Jane, but he just smiled and continued calling me Mrs. Bob.

The next morning I didn't feel well, and had been throwing up. I wasn't sure if it was morning sickness or a virus. I knew what was expected so I dragged myself out of bed and finally managed to get dressed and dress Mandy for the 9:00 a.m. session. I went into the nursery to leave her but no one showed up to keep the nursery. The pastor's wife finally came in about 10:00 a.m. for that session. Mandy had just messed her clothes up so I went back to the trailer to get her some more clothes and took them to the nursery and changed her. It was about 10:10 a.m. I walked in and looked for Bob and he was sitting with a friend of ours on the second row. I noticed the church was full as I walked down the isle and took my place beside Bob. The pastor was talking, rambling or something, making announcements. Then he began saying remarks that directly related to me. "You can't trust a missionary on the field if they can't show up for services on time." he said. "These missionary wives who think they can just go in and out of the services any time they please can not be trusted." he criticized. He went on for what seemed like fifteen minutes on how terrible I was. I sat there in tears humiliated to death. Sam patted my knees and said, "Don' worry about it sister, he's crazy." Bob on the other hand who thinks no wrong of anyone said, "Honey, he's not talking about you." but every one else knew he was.

After that I got Mandy and went to the trailer and told Bob that I was not going back into that church again. Bob kept saying that I was too sensitive and that he wasn't saying that because of me, but Sam convinced Bob that I was right and that it was gross ignorance for a man to do such a thing as embarrassing as that. I did not think it being ignorance as much as he was just a big jerk; an egotistical one at that. Bob just did not want to believe anyone could be that cruel and insensitive. The pastor never said a word as we packed up and drove off in the distance.

I wish we had the wisdom and boldness back then to deal with jerks, but we were still young and inexperienced. (*May the Lord repay him according to his works.* II Timothy 4:14) We can forgive them but we do not have to allow them to continue to abuse us. In fact it is wise to avoid them at all cost.

We drove about eight hours to Jacksonville, where Bob's brother resided. He lived in a gorgeous, Spanish style home with a swimming pool in a rich development. We stayed until I became a nervous wreck chasing Mandy all over the house popping her hands for touching things. After three days I had enough and convinced Bob that we needed to go home. We had a meeting in Georgia on a Wednesday night so we left early that morning. The meeting went well. They handed us a check for fifty dollars for a love offering for coming and sharing our burden. We felt very blessed to have such a large love offering. Bob was embarrassed but had to ask the pastor if they could give us cash instead because we were flat broke and had no food or gas. He was nice about it but had to go to some trouble to get it. He took us out to eat and sent us on our way. We drove half the night to get home very exhausted.

A week later we received a letter from the pastor of the church that supported us ten dollars a month in Pensacola. The letter said that they felt "lead of the Lord" to drop our support. Then we received a bill for four hundred and fifty dollars for the expense we incurred on that trip. It took us months to pay for that meeting in Florida. We often thought of quitting. Was all this worth it? It was hard to resist getting bitter toward people that treated us this way. Some how we managed to keep our eyes on the Lord and tried to overlook how stupid people could be.

Bob thought we should take a survey trip to see where the Lord was leading us. The church that had contacted our mission board earlier was anxious for us to visit, so we planned a trip to Italy. The church in Italy let our board know that they had a group of Italians that were saved and they needed a pastor. Our plan was to find out as much as we could to help us raise the support we needed. It seemed that missionaries who had visited their field of work got their support sooner. We had been on deputation already two years and were getting weary of the expense. It took all of our support to live and to travel and we had no designated funds for this trip or any money for passage and outfitting, but we managed to save enough to book our flight for November. We contacted the Dean of Women and her husband to let them know of our progress since they were always interested in what was going on in our lives. They told us of a couple that had previously attended the college who was now missionaries in Italy as well. We contacted them since they lived in Rome and they were able to meet us as we arrived.

When we arrived in Rome, Ross met us at the airport. We were complete strangers but felt the warmth of their friendship immediately. But that was the only warmth we grasped. The house was freezing. I wore typical clothing for America, a dress, hose and a lightweight coat. It was forty degrees outside and the same inside the house. I did not know if I would survive. The next day they took us to our destination, the train station. We were going to Naples where the Military church had arranged for us to be picked up. We were starved because we could not speak the language enough to even get a piece of pizza. The gentleman who picked us up was very religious. He prayed when we arrived and thanked God for the safe trip, which was fine. But then he proceeded to pray four more times on the way back to the military housing. Not that I am against praying, but if you close your eyes in Naples you might get robbed blind.

For the week we stayed in Naples we were shifted from one house to another. They took us to meet this Italian and that one, and to stay with several different American families. The roads were so rough it was a miracle that I did not lose the baby within me. All the jiggling and bumping was miserable and no one seemed to eat. I did survive however, I wondered how though. On Thanksgiving Day we were loaded up and taken back to the train station without breakfast. The smells of Thanksgiving dinner pierced my nose and I was so hungry. We missed the train and waited for hours before we could find the right train to be on. Nothing to eat all day long and I was also exhausted from the trip and being pregnant. When we arrived in Rome we had to call the Stumps but had no special coin to do so. Bob finally purchased a piece of cold pizza so we could get the change we needed to make our call. Ross told us how to get out to their house, two buses and a short hike of a mile or two or rather it seemed like it. They were waiting up for us when we finally arrived at 11:00 p.m. "Too bad you weren't here for lunch. We had a great Thanksgiving lunch. We don't have anything left. Are you hungry? If so, I 'll see if I can find you something."

"No thanks, we are tired." We excused ourselves and went to the cold bed.

The next day we rested for the trip back home. The following day, Ross returned us to the airport, and we boarded the plane. We noticed the plane was so full of men, lots of men. A stewardess told us that the men were off of an oil rig in Saudi Arabia and were on their way home in the States. They became loud and disorderly. I had never seen so much drinking going on. We joked that we were a flying bar room, and the only thing that kept God from destroying the plane was us. The men finally either passed out or went to sleep. They did not even wake up for the landing, and when the pilot almost overshot the runway and had to slam on breaks, skidded a bit, several of the men came flying out of their seats rolling down the isle. It was a rough landing. I was so glad to get off the plane. We often wondered if the pilot was drunk as well. You never know.

CHAPTER XI

WINGS OF FAITH

༶

Psalms 40:5 *Many, O Lord, my God, are thy wonderful works which thou hast done, and thy thoughts which are toward us: they cannot be reckoned up in order unto thee. If I would declare and speak of them they are more than can be numbered.*

Bob was excited and encouraged by going to Italy on that little trip and told the pastor at the Military Church that we would definitely be coming to Naples to work with the Italian people. They told us that about nine hundred to a thousand dollars a month was what we need to live on in that area, that it should be more than enough to meet our needs and we were half way there. Once you got half of your support the rest seemed to come in quicker.

The winter of 1978-79 seemed long. Meetings were extremely difficult to book again and the weather was unusually cold and bad. Our little trailer was hard to heat. We had a blizzard that year, and the snow blew in the window cracks.

As my due date approached for our second child to be born, we were concerned where we would put her. We knew the basinet would last for a couple of months and after that we thought about using a drawer for her until she turned over. In our rather small accommodations there just was not room to put another bed or child for that matter. Then the pastor offered us the use of the church house. Our church had just completed Sunday school rooms in the new educational wing, and would not be needing the Church house anymore. We were thrilled to hear of the move we could make in a couple months.

On April 4th our second child, Brooke was born. Only this time I was not put to sleep, and had her with an epidural. The night before the C-Section, I dreamed that the doctor forgot to do the tubule ligation. There was no way I wanted to get pregnant and have another child in Italy. The doctor agreed that with my age, having any more than two C-Sections was not advisable. As he was doing the procedure, I reminded him that I wanted the tubule legations and I told him that I had a dream that he forgot to do it. He just laughed. Within minutes they pulled Brooke out and cleaned her up wrapped her in a blanket and handed her to Bob. It was a much better experience being awake for this birth. The beauty of this experience was that Bob got to hold her for an hour, while they worked on me. I could not take my eyes off the dark eyed, black haired, chunky infant. She lay so quite in her daddy's arms. Truly we had been blessed again with a miracle from God.

Five weeks later we moved from our little cracker box to the seemingly big beige house, which was about two hundred and fifty yards away. This was to be our fifth move in the four years we had been married. But I didn't mind since we really needed the space. Shortly, I was traveling with Bob again although it was a little more difficult. We could still use the travel trailer and that made going with him easier. I would pack the trailer and did not have to unpack until we came home. I was so grateful that my parents allowed us to use it as much as we did.

We had many miles yet to travel and this time we headed north. We had friends we often traveled with and every time Sam would hear of a meeting somewhere we would plan together. This time we were going to New London, Ohio. A mission's conference was scheduled there and the pastor had invited us up. The people were so friendly and very kind and when we arrived the pastor said we could park our trailers out at their school about four miles away. We set up camp and enjoyed being near to an inside bathroom.

The weather had been a little uncertain and there had been storms that week. Ohio seemed to have rougher weather than we were used to in North Carolina. When we got out of church that evening there had been some wind and rain, but the forecast for the night was predicted to be somewhat dangerous with possible tornadoes. We had been in those situations before in another part of Ohio, when tornadoes were all around us and by the grace of God they missed the trailer.

We went to sleep, but around 1:00 a.m. it started raining extremely hard. It woke us up and we were concerned if that was the line of storms we had heard about. We turned the radio on trying to find a local station when we heard Sam call out to us. They too had been alarmed at the raging storm. We were hollering out to each other through the doors when we began to hear the roaring sound like a train coming. Both Bob and Sam began to figure out where we could take cover. We knew the school was nothing but a mere aluminum building. I started grabbing the girls and Bob and started out the door when we heard the horn of the train. Thank God it was a train instead of a tornado touching down. It took a while to calm down and I don't think we slept at all that night.

Other meetings were further into Ohio. All the people we met were so kind and nice. One of the churches took all the missionaries and purchased a suit for the men and some ladies from the church took us ladies shopping. They gave each of us twenty-five dollars to spend. So we did witness people who were loving and generous. After that we went to Indiana. While we were there we heard of a meeting in Texas. That was so very far away, but Sam thought it would be a good opportunity to get support. They were going to Brazil and needed more support also.

Bob did not feel good about going to Texas. Later he wished he had trusted his intuition. When we got there the mission's conference turned out to be a gospel singing. They were mean and ugly to us and the meetings turned out to be a take off on missionaries. We had now been in several meetings in the south that the title of the mission's conferences should have been "What is wrong with missionaries?" Needless to say we did not stay long, but it was a very long trip back home. I think Bob drove it all in one day and night. We did not have the money to stop and spend the night anywhere.

It was not surprising that Bob had grown restless with deputation and announced that as soon as he got enough money he was going to buy our tickets to Italy. We were receiving almost eight hundred dollars a month support now and was encouraged with God's provisions. However, I was reluctant to go at that time since we had no passage and no money to purchase any furniture when we arrived.

We prayed for the money to come in for the plane fare and behold, a church provided the funds for our tickets. Bob was so excited as we prayed, "God we are trusting you to get us there and provide what we need." And he purchased our tickets from New York to Rome, Italy for October 9, 1979 leaving at 7:00 p.m.

As the saying goes."...this put the nail in their coffin...." and our parents realized that we were really leaving. It had been a long time since we knew what God wanted us to do, because the process took four years. They thought we were crazy. The thought of losing not only their children, but now their grandchildren to the mission field was more than they were ready to deal with. There were many tears and broken hearts although we all knew that God was in control and that He had a job for us to do. God would provide but it was difficult for our parents to see how, and sometimes us as well.

Many times I would question, "What are we going to do for furniture, we have no money to purchase even a stove to cook on?" Bob said he did not care if we had to sit on crates and eat off the floor; this deputation was for the birds. It was time for us go.

There was so much to do and so many people to say goodbye to, papers to get into order and passports to acquire. We had no idea about any of the things that had to be done. And what could we ship: when, where, how, and the cost had to be figured. Well, the "how" was our biggest quest. We had only eight weeks to be in New York. We prayed and made phone calls and then one day my father had suggested that we contact a shipping company that was owned by R. J. Reynolds. Bob found the contact number after some research and talked to the manager responsible for the overseas shipping in New York. Bob talked to him about our unique set of circumstances and why we were going to Italy and the man said he would get back in touch with us as soon as possible. We prayed again and waited.

Three weeks before we were to leave we still did not know how we were getting to New York to catch the plane. At first my parents said they would take us, but backed out and said it would be too difficult to say goodbye there. Then it happened again. I woke up with my head swimming. Here I was with packing to do and a lot going on and I was dizzy again. It was much worse this time and every time I lifted my head off the pillow I would throw up. This time the doctor said it was a virus. After several days I began to show signs of improvement, and resumed my packing and taking care of the children.

The manager of Sea Land called us and said yes, they would be glad to ship anything we wanted to send to Italy and all our household belongings for one dollar. They would have a tractor trailer in front of our house and within a few days and they did. They left it for forty-eight hours while we loaded it with tons of stuff. About ten men in the church showed up to pack the truck so it only took one day to load. After everyone had left we stood around looking at the empty house with the big glass windows in the living room. Our voices echoed though out the house as we walked around trying to grasp the moment and finishing the packing of our suitcases. We took everything we had and then some. They came back and took the tractor trailer truck to Wilmington and shipped it to Naples, Italy. We knew God worked miracles but this was more than we could ask or comprehend.

We made final arrangements to fly to New York but did not know how we were going to pay for our tickets. One afternoon we received a call from a good friend, "Our class would like for you to come before you leave and bring the children so we can have a farewell party for you." We went to the party and the class had cake and played with Mandy and Brooke. These first graders brought out a jar of coins and presented it to us and said they had been saving money for us for a long time and would like to help us get to Italy. We wept as later we counted the money and it was to the dollar the exact amount of money we needed to pay for the trip to New York. Again, and again God had supplied and showed us His faithfulness to us and it encouraged us daily to trust Him more.

Then the day arrived for us to leave for New York. We had decided to leave on October eighth since our Rome flight would leave at 7:00 p.m. on the ninth. With the emotion involved we somehow knew it would be very hard to fly the entire trip in one day. All our friends from the church, brothers and sisters, other relatives, pastors and finally our parents were all at the airport to say goodbye. I held my mom tight and she and I cried and cried some more.... like babies. I grabbed my father as if I would never see him again and my heart broke. How much more did my Heavenly Father's heart break when he sent His son, on that first mission's trip into this world to tell us of His love? We boarded the plane and I cried all the way to New York.

Great flight, a good night's sleep and the next morning I was filled with anticipation. I had talked again to my parents; I did not know when I would get to talk to them again. The girls were playing around the room with toys I brought when Bob broke out in a song. It was out of character for him, but someone had to sing "Happy Birthday" to him. How could I have forgotten his birthday? With my emotions on edge, once again I broke out in tears. But he forgave me and thought it was funny enough to still make jokes about thirty years later.

CHAPTER XII

ITALY, THE CONCRETE JUNGLE

꙳

Matt: 6:20 *But lay up for yourselves treasures in heaven, where neither moth nor rust doth corrupt and where thieves do not break through nor steal;*

Philippians 1:29 *For unto you it is given in the behalf of Christ, not only to believe on him but also to suffer for his sake,*

It was a very long tiring trip, but the girls did great. The Stumps were gracious again to pick us up at the airport. They took us in, fed us, befriended us, and helped us make contact with the right authorities. You can say they took us under their experienced wings and guided us to everything that had to be done about registering in the country. We made contact with the military pastor to let him know we had arrived. They had a change in pastors but someone would be picking us up within a few days.

Amanda and Brooke did well although they were so young. Mandy was two years old and Brooke was six months. I was still nursing Brooke so she wasn't eating much food yet. Cheri and Criss, the Stumps' children, seemed to love the girls right off and helped me with watching them. I had remembered how cold it was in Italy so I brought plenty of warm clothes for them and they did not seem to mind the house being chilly. Brooke slept with us and Mandy took right up with Cheri and slept with her. I felt better about the arrangement because I knew they would stay warmer that way.

The next week the Morgans arrived to take us to Naples. We did not know who these people were. They were not military. We quickly found out that they were the missionaries who were also asked to come to the same area by the same pastor that asked us and about four other missionary families to come for the same work. This presented a sensitive issue among us even on the road back to Naples. The pastor who caused this problem was no longer in Naples. There was nothing we could do except to accept it and try to work together although there were some differences of approach we would have with the people.

We were extremely grateful that the military church was taking us in and helping us to get settled into a house. They provided a small section of an apartment for us in the upstairs of their church building. The apartment was used as part of their nursery during Church. They had set up a bedroom and a small kitchen in two of the rooms, but it was a place we could stay until our furniture arrived and we could find a place to live.

It did not take us long to suspect some real problems in the American church. All the people wanted to talk about were demons and people who were demon possessed. They were looking for a demon under every rock. There were stories floating around of a girl in the church who was crawling on her belly like a snake, hissing and demons spoke out of her mouth. If the lights went out, which they often did in Naples, it was because of some demons in the church building. They talked about witnessing to sailors on the docks and some sailors claimed to be demons. We had never been exposed to such evil activity in all our lives. The force of evil prevailed and we could feel the oppression not only there among the Satan hunters, but in Italy as a whole.

Mandy had not adjusted well to the new culture, and Brooke was too young to notice at six months old. Mandy cried very often. She seemed to be fearful and clung to me especially if Italians were present. She had been potty trained for six months but also had started wetting the bed at night. I dismissed it and thought it was just a change for her and it would take time for her to adjust. But one Sunday, I went to the nursery to check on Brooke, and I noticed a lady talking very sternly to a child, "Don't you know that if you died you will go to hell, and you would not see your daddy and mommy again? Now don't you want to go to heaven? You don't want to go to hell, do you? The devil is in hell and he is bad and there is fire there, now don't you want Jesus in your heart?" I looked over the half-door to see that it was my Mandy she had cornered and was talking to. I became furious that she was talking to my child like that and told her not to speak to my child again like that. I told her that Mandy was only two years old and that she was not capable of comprehending those concepts at this age. How could people be so insensitive? She insisted that the pastor told her to tell each child the plan of salvation, but this was not His plan. It was scare tactics. I was not opposed to teaching a child the plan of salvation if it is done in a way that the child is not afraid but this was abusive to scare a child like this. I forbade her to speak again to Mandy about salvation.

The Morgans were nice to take us around to look for places to rent and we looked for weeks. We also had to purchase a car. Our church gave us almost two thousand dollars to help us out once we got to Italy and we knew we would have to find a car with those funds. After we had looked we found an old car that would suit our needs.

Since the Italians were very familiar with Americans in the area, it was not hard to find someone in real estate who spoke English to help us find a house. This man found houses for Americans all the time. He took us to three places. I did not particularly care for any of them. He said he did not know of anything else in the area so we took the last place he showed us. The other two places were totally out because of the location and danger to the children.

It was another couple of weeks when our furniture arrived and we moved into the isolated house in the country on the tenth of December. Our landlord's house was across the street set back off the road. It had been an old barn they had converted into a house. Their house was dirty, old and cold. It appeared to be from the seventeenth century. We spoke to the landlord through the realtor who interpreted for us. We asked if we could install a kerosene heater in the house since it had no heating system. He sat at his table with his coat on throwing scraps out the open door in forty degree weather and wanted to know why we needed heat. We could not make him understand why but he agreed that we could put a hole in the wall for a vent if we would fix it back when we left.

Our furniture arrived and we were happy to be out of the apartment at last. As you entered the door you only saw an extremely long hallway. The first room on the right was a nice size living room with velvety red and white wall paper with a fireplace in the corner. Bob's office was next on the right and the children's bedroom was the last room on the right. At the very end of the hallway was the bathroom. The dinning room with French doors to the front porch and kitchen were the next two rooms on the left with our bedroom being the last room on the left, just across the hall from the children's. We had a beautiful gated yard with palm trees all around the property. The way the house was laid out, the only rooms we could use were our bedrooms and the kitchen because the rest of the house was too cold to use. We did build a fire occasionally in the living room, but most of the time we stayed in the kitchen.

There was always so much to do just to maintain everyday life. I had no washer or dryer for the clothes, so I washed clothes by hand in the bathtub. Diapers were especially hard to get clean. (Imagine that!) The clothes would take days sometimes to dry on racks I would put in the dining room. Occasionally I would have to re-wash the clothes because of the dampness; they would just hang and start smelling musty. Everything stayed dusty and dirty. I had to sweep and mop at least twice a day. Cooking was a chore as well. I would have to cook everything from scratch. There were no frozen vegetables, no pre-prepared foods at all. We ate pasta everyday. I could not even find baby food so Brooke went straight from nursing to spaghetti. By the time I got lunch cleaned up and the girls' naps it was time for supper. Needless to say I lost weight during this time.

On the front porch of the house, the owner had a statue of Mary place in the wall. It had a light that stayed on twenty-four hours a day. We called it a god shelf, and we did not like it. What would be the harm if we took it down since we do not believe in worshipping saints? But we found out that the statue was very important to Mrs. Fontana. She had a fit and made us put the statue of Mary back up as she was adamant that Mary protected the house and that we should put it back up or move. So we put it back up. We knew that it was no more than a piece of concrete that could not hear or see.

Everything was so strange, so different. It seemed like we had landed on another planet. There were dirty looking people, and trash everywhere. There was a huge lake we had to go around to get to the church which was said to have been a sunken city. Some said it was a volcano. We had to drive twenty-five miles to the grocery store and along the way trash was piled four feet high. Beside the road stood prostitutes and transvestites typically known as the camp fire girls by the military people because they stood by burning tires at night. There were new sights, sounds and smells everywhere we went. In the Naples area alone there were twelve volcanoes, and one that was occasionally active known as Vesuvius. The bay of Naples, Capri, ancient ruins, boiling lava, sulfur steam coming from the side of a mountain, islands, grottos in the ocean, all was amazing to me. I never got tired of seeing all that God had created. Naples was truly a beautiful place. Sometimes it was also referred to as the cesspool of the world. It was dirty and nasty. One time I heard that there were more rats under the streets than people above.

It was time to prepare for our first Christmas in Italy. I knew it would be lonesome and there would not be the familiar things around so I had packed Christmas presents for the girls and all that we needed to make things seems like home. As soon as we had settled in the house, we went to the grocery store to purchase our month's supply of food. In thinking about Christmas dinner, I chose a plump chicken which I put in the freezer until Christmas Eve.

We found a little 4 foot Christmas tree in downtown Naples, but it was exceptionally hard to locate and very expensive for our small budget. Seems like we found some lights at the large department store downtown and we had some decorations we had brought from home. Christmas Eve after the girls went to sleep we set their things out around the tree. We had brought an indoor wooden slide, a couple of infant toys for Brooke and a doll for Mandy. Our intentions were not to teach the girls about Santa Clause, so we never mentioned that he brought toys or gifts for them. We just did not feel comfortable about teaching them to believe in Santa, so we brought them up knowing that the gifts came from us.

Christmas morning was uneventful until I noticed that the chicken had it head still on. I hollered for Bob to come. He told me that he would cut it off for me. I was a city girl and I had never encountered a chicken intact. All my chickens had no heads, no insides and no feet. When the chicken fully thawed, I turned it over and not only did the head flop out, but the feet were there as well, then I noticed that the chicken had never been cleaned and I had froze it that way.

"Bob, you're going to have to cut the feet off too!" I exclaimed.

"Hey, I told you I would cut the head off, you can do the rest!" He said.

"But Bob, I don't know how to clean this chicken," again I protested.

"All you got to do is reach up there inside and pull all that stuff out."

"I can't, I'll throw up, Bob!" I said.

This was just the beginning of what I was to learn to do. I finally cut the back of the chicken and took a spoon and scraped all the guts out. "There," I said to myself. "I figured that out."

The pastor of the American church was younger and we had often heard him and his wife argue when they lived in the apartment beside us when we lived in the church apartment. He often preached about being a member of the local church closest to you and that it was sin if you didn't. We just could not agree with that. We were there for the Italians not for the American church. The odd thing about his messages was that we were the only ones who were not members with that church. Sometimes he would have a lengthy invitation, waiting on us to join. It was humiliating and embarrassing and I would have crawled under my seat if I could. This went on for a month or more and one Sunday after church was over, the pastor called the head deacon and said there would be a business meeting. My heart sank, for I just knew that they were going to ask us to leave the church or bring us before the people and humiliate us for not joining their church. They were supporting us financially so they would probably stop that as well. Instead, the deacon stood before the people and asked the pastor to leave while they took a vote of confidence. In so many words they wanted to see how many people wanted to keep him as pastor. Everyone was shocked as the pastor called out, "I'll not have that, I resign as of this moment." He walked out and went back to the States within two weeks.

We became friends with the Morgans and their children as we worked together gathering the Italians for services. We also had some language classes with them. We did notice that the Americans within the military church treated us differently than they did the Morgans. They would take them to the military commissary, purchase things for them, buy them groceries, take them to the military park, invite them out for meals and invite them to their homes. They treated us like we had a plague. Many times it would hurt us, but we kept it in our heart and considered that they truly did not understand that our mission was with the Italians. We wanted to live like them, associate with them, and give them the gospel.

The American church was in contact with a saved Italian man who lived in Sicily, which would come to Naples once a month to preach the gospel. Our jobs were to visit the Italians, give them encouragement and get them to the meetings once a month. Some of the Italians had come to know the Lord through Vince's ministry. He had a passion for his people. We had about twenty who came to the meetings every month. One dear sweet Christian lady was Mrs. Deanna. She would talk to the others about the Lord and encourage them to trust in Christ instead of the Catholic Church.

Being all alone in the country wasn't extremely bad. Although I was lonely for family, the Lord filled my life with many things to do. Bob was gone a lot visiting with Mr.

Morgan and taking some Italian lessons. It became too much for me to try to learn the language with the girls, so I just stayed at home. Every afternoon while they were napping the landlord's daughters would come to my house and they found it intriguing to try to teach me new words in Italian. I thought it was fun as well as it was someone to be with. We had a great time together although the communication was terrible. Sometimes they would teach me how to cook new and interesting things and bring me bread they had made. I tried to make bread the way they did but failed each time. They would ask me what I did to make it go bad and finally I understood that I was killing the yeast by using boiling hot water instead of warm water to dissolve the yeast.

We had been in Italy about four months and our support level was very low. It was clear to us that we had been misinformed about the support level we needed. The Military church had informed us that nine hundred dollars would be sufficient but failed to recognize that was if you were Military. They did not have to live off the Italian economy. On the other hand the Morgans had about nineteen hundred dollars a month support.

February was an unusually low month. I would get so upset and would worry myself to death trying to figure out how we were going to make it each month. This month I cried and was so afraid we would not make it. You would think that God had moved off the throne and left us empty handed. When we got the check cashed we organized and separated the money in envelopes as to how we could make a plan work to stretch our money. Gas was four dollars and twenty-five cents a gallon, hamburger was about four dollars a pound and everything else was so expensive. We paid the rent, about three hundred and fifty dollars and divided the rest in envelopes for groceries, so much for gas in another envelope, so much for the rent in another envelope, so much for fire wood and kerosene in another envelope and ended up with about five or six envelopes. I put them in the freezer because we had heard of Americans being robbed all the time. Not only would they steal from the Americans but they would steal from their own mother if she turned her back. But Bob did not like the money in the freezer; after a few days he took it out because he said it was getting soggy, and he put it in his desk drawer. The next week a man came to the house to deliver fire wood and Bob went back to the desk to get the money while he stood at the door.

Occasionally, Bob got to preach in the American Church. He always did a great job delivering the message, one that was encouraging and uplifting. Bob was an expository preacher; that was the way he was trained. This Sunday night he preached from I Peter 2:21 to 25 on *"What It Means To Suffer For Christ."* Christ left us an example to follow and that is one of suffering. On the way home we talked about how we had not really suffered as the early Christians had suffered. We had never been thrown in prison, or beaten, or lost our families. We had not been called to be a martyr for Him, for which we were so grateful.

When we drove up to the house, there was something appeared unusually strange. The light on the porch we left on was not on. As we approached the door it was plain to see that someone had taken an ax to the door, but was unable to enter that way. I glanced to the left where we had French doors and they were swung open with the glass knocked out. Our hearts raced as we entered the house. All the lights in the house had been turned on and the house was a wreck. The clothes were dumped on the floor, and all the money we had was gone. The jewelry box had been stripped of all our jewelry including my diamond and our class rings. My heart was torn out. How could this have happened? How were we going to make it through the month now? I wanted to scream out to God, "Where were you, God?"

We went down to our landlord's to call the police. Bob told them we had been robbed. They talked on the phone like they would be right out, but they never showed up. The next day Bob called them back and they simply said that they could not do anything.

We only had five dollars in our pocket that night. We drove over to the Morgans house so we could call the States to ask my parents if they could send us some money. It took about two hours to get through to the operator in Rome. I was crying as I told my parents what had happened and asked them to contact our home church and let them know as well. It was a terrible feeling as we drove back home and I cried most of the night. My parents were going to wire us some money the church was sending us and said they would wire it to the Bank of Naples. After they had talked to American Express they told them the money would be there the following day. We drove twenty-five miles to the bank but they did not have the money. Then I had to go by myself because Bob was busy with the ministry. I drove back the next day and the next day, but still no money had arrived. Each time my head was spinning, but I learned to drive with it like that. Five days I had gone to Naples and they did not know what we were talking about. We called my parents back, and they were upset that the money that they had sent had not arrived. They called to get more money wired and related that the first money was not there. The bank gave them the name of the president of the bank so they could send it directly to him. We waited for two days and went back to the bank and asked to speak to the president of the bank and gave them the name that the Bank in New York had given my parents, but he had not been at the bank in several years. We asked if we could see the president and explained our situation. After we waited for an hour they finally agreed to let us talk to the President. A guard led us through long marble halls and up marble stairs through another large hall incased with marble statues everywhere. We entered this room with twenty foot ceilings and there sat a distinguished looking man behind a desk. Needless to say we felt out of place.

He was very polite to us as he introduced himself in English. We were relieved that we would not have to struggle to tell him why we were there. Bob explained our predicament and our reason for being in Italy, but he thought we were asking the bank for money. Finally, we explained again and he finally understood us. We gave him a tract and we had the opportunity to witness to him as he asked questions about our faith in Christ. We all went downstairs to see what had become of the money sent. The first wired money had just arrived. He gave that to us and assured us that when the second time it was wired, it would be sent back.

God was using this entire situation not only to teach us what it meant to suffer for Him, but to bring the Gospel to one who would not have had the opportunity to hear it otherwise. It took our robbery to get the message of salvation to this high official in the largest bank in Naples, Italy. We truly felt like ambassadors, "an official representative of the highest rank, accredited by one government to another," Bob would so often quote from the dictionary.

My mom often sent things to Italy for us. One time I told her it would be nice next time if she would send some grits. I missed having grits, but she sent two large bags of instant grits. I hated instant grits, so I had set them on top of the kitchen cabinets. I did not know what I was going to even do with them, but thanked my mother graciously that she had spent so much money sending them to us. She would also send candy for the girls and some clothes although our packages had been gone through and some things missing by the time we got them.

During the next few months when our income was so low we could not buy much I would often cry when we got our check. But each month God proved Himself faithful and

I would thank Him. The next month the same thing occurred and I would cry again. I was so afraid God would let us down, but He never did. Even when our food ran out and there was no money, I pulled those big round containers off the top of the cabinet and we ate instant grits for a week.

As I look back and think how ungrateful I was to have the grits. I was worse than Elijah sitting under the Juniper Tree, weltering in self-pity again. I even refused to thank God for the food that week. I was ashamed of myself and asked for forgiveness for the way I was acting. God provided our needs just like he promised. More than that He was humbling us to be more like Himself.

CHAPTER XIII

THE LANDLORD'S DAUGHTER

⌣∶⌣

Acts 26:18 *"To open their eyes, and to turn them from darkness to light and from the power of Satan unto God, that they may receive forgiveness of sin, and inheritance among them who are sanctified by faith that is in me."*

Lena and Pupa, our landlord's daughters, continued to visit and asked me to visit them. I went down to their house and I was fascinated at how they lived. The only heat was a fireplace in the den/dining room for the two story house. Cats and dogs ran in and out all the time, flies everywhere and cats in the fireplace to keep warm. They made their own sausage, had chicken and ducks and pigs in the back part of the house. Sometimes they had a huge tub boiling in the fireplace filled with pig skin and bones. They would boil it for many hours and pour the lard in the pig's bladder and hang it out back.

The girls had begun coming to the Italian services with us and they listened well. Lena was serious about wanting to find out more about God. On Easter we invited them to come to the Easter Sun Rise services with us at the American church. I knew they would not be able to understand, but the Holy Spirit could work in their hearts. Lena was the only one who went with us. She had such a great attitude and seemed to want to know more each time she had the opportunity to be with us. A week later Vince was back for another service. Lena and Pupa both attended this time. At the end of the service when the invitation was held, Lena was crying. I knew the Spirit of God was convicting her. Mrs. Deanna went up to her and asked her to trust the Lord for her salvation. But Lena just stood there, crying and shaking, speechless. She turned to me and said, "Please be my friend and help me." I told her I was her friend but I could not help her that only God could help. She seemed so distraught when we took them home. Pupa did not say a word. She appeared to be angry about the idea that Lena was sensitive to God.

The next day, I had not heard from Lena so I went down to her house. I really had a burden to see Lena saved and felt like she was close to making that decision. When I entered the room several people were there including her mother who was a very strong traditionalist of the Roman Catholic faith. Someone drove up and everyone went running out the door, that is everyone except Lena and me. She pulled me into the kitchen and tears started streaming down her face. I saw the desperation on her face as she begged me to help her. She said her heart was so heavy and she was so miserable and I saw that she was broken. I told her that I could do nothing for her except to pray. Only He could heal her feelings of pain and burden. I told her I could not save her, only God could and that she needed to pray and ask Him for forgiveness of sin, as she continued to beg me to help her. I told her I loved her and again reminded her to pray to God.

I was rejoicing in my heart that Lena was so tender to God and I felt that she would make that decision to pray and repent. I did not know if she understood what I said but she acted like she did. I had such a language struggle, and I knew very little Italian. But what I could not say in English the Holy Spirit did the work. Two days later, Lena and Pupa came by. I had to be careful not to mention anything about the Lord in front of Pupa. She had seemed resentful about Lena's interest in the gospel and us talking about the Lord. But while she was being distracted by Mandy in her room playing, Lena took me to the living room and shut the door. She told me that she had prayed and accepted God and He had filled her heart with such tremendous peace. She had peace and contentment on her face as she was smiling and telling me how she had prayed and how the burden of sin left. I rejoiced with her. She asked for a song book, the songs in her language she had never heard before the meetings that filled her soul with joy and happiness. I gave Lena a song book and a Bible of her own and Bob wrote in the front of the Bible, the date of her salvation. We were so thrilled to see God's purpose of our being in not only His will but in Italy.

It was strange that Lena and Pupa did not return that week, very strange. They had come everyday to our house for conversation and now we had not seen them. Bob and I talked about going to see her, but felt something was going on and thought it better if we stayed away. It was the following week that Lena showed up at our house, alone. She said that her mother made her bring the song book and Bible back. They had forbidden her to see us again and she was to have nothing to do with the church. She asked as tears streamed down her face, "Can I have the page that Bob recorded my salvation date? They can take away my Bible and song book, but they can not take it out of my heart!"

Lena was not allowed to see us again. Her family sent her away to her sister's house on the other side of Naples. Why were these people so ignorant? I wept bitter tears that Satan tried to put an end to Lena's belief in God, but like she said, nothing could remove it from her heart not even

Satan. He had blinded the eyes of these precious people. I hated the Catholic Church even more for keeping the Italian people ignorant to the Word of God. I took a long walk in the field to be alone with God and prayed for Lena until my heart felt like it was breaking. Oh how blessed I was to have the freedom to believe and to worship God. I knew that Lena would need His presence and asked God to comfort her and to help her through this awful time.

One afternoon, the realtor, who had showed us the house, came by. He said he wanted to see how we were doing, but his conversation led to a much different reason for him being there. He said he had been sent to warn us to leave Lena alone, and that if we did not leave her alone, that Mr. Fontana usually settled these matters with a gun. He said that it would be advisable if we could find another place to live. So we started looking. We really did not know how serious to take these people. When we went to Lena's house to give her father our thirty day notice to move, everyone in the family was there and they asked why? Her mother and father acted like they were shocked that we were going to move. We told them that Mr. Fontana had sent the realtor to our house and that we had been told to move. He denied ever sending anyone to tell us that, but we had already secured another house fifteen miles away.

In July 1980, we moved into a large house in Castel Volturno. It was very nice by Italian standards. The house itself was on the upper level. There was a basement underneath, but it was like the first floor and it was all open. It had a large gated yard which our dog Elsa enjoyed. She was our guard dog. After we were robbed, someone suggested that we get a dog, that Italians were afraid of dogs. She was a big boxer who was going to be put to sleep because the military couple who owned her could not find her a home and did not have the money yet to have her euthanized. They were planning to return to the states and could not take her with them.

No one ever suspected that she could never hurt a flea. She looked mean, but the girls were all over her and she never even growled. She did kill a couple of foxes, and a rat and barked at the snakes, but she loved intimidating people. And she did keep the place secure, but we were also advised to get a watchman. It was contrary to our American way of thinking and our belief that God would keep us safe, but we did pay the watchman twenty dollars a month to get the word out that we did not want to be robbed. I guess you could say we paid the mafia to keep our home from being robbed. This is how the mafia works, you pay to stay safe.

This house was hard to keep clean and there was a lot to do to maintain it. For one thing the well water was not drinkable because it had high levels of arsenic. We were told we could bath in it if we put a gallon of bleach in the well every month.

City water was inside the gate but it was not plumbed into the house. I had to go down to the faucet every day and fill a five gallon jug of water for cooking and bring it upstairs, about twenty-five steps. The house was impressive with its beautiful tile floors, but the kitchen was terribly drab with red and black tile on the floor and twelve foot tall walls. In the winter the house was freezing and our kerosene heater did very little good at all. There was a breeze in the house when it was windy outside. The warmest it got in the winter with the kerosene heater going full force was fifty-five degrees. The only way we could stay halfway warm at all was to put on layers and layers of clothing and insulated underclothes. We usually stayed in the ugly kitchen where we ran a little kerosene heater. With cooking, it would stay half way comfortable in there. We moved our couch in there and we lived in the fifteen by twenty foot kitchen day and night, which got very tiring at times. The master bath was huge and tiled from floor to ceiling with navy blue tile. It was beautiful, however if you even walked in there you left prints everywhere. I would have to clean it several times a day and almost went crazy trying to keep it clean. The other bath was brown and small, but was less trouble to keep clean. I remember one time the element went out on the hot water heater which was hanging on the wall six foot off the floor. Bob and I thought, no big deal we can do this. He found the right plug to take out and all of a sudden water started gushing out. It must have been a fifty gallon tank, because we were trying to catch the water, which was still extremely warm, in five gallon buckets and pouring it out in the shower and commode as fast as we could. The water was so hot it was making the plastic buckets limp and hard to handle. That was some comical experience. We laughed until we cried.

Nothing in that house worked properly. We had a power cord that ran from a building our landlord owned across the street to the house. That was how we got power, but it was somewhat low voltage. Imagine plugging your entire house electrical needs to an extension cord. That is exactly what we had.

Bob decided to fix the power so we could have more voltage. I call him *Tim the tool man*, because he does not have the skills for that sort of thing. He thought the power was off, in which I suppose I relayed the wrong message and he was shocked once when he got between the cabinets and the refrigerator and touched the two hundred twenty voltage wire and could not get loose. I finally saw what was happening when he was banging his head between the cabinet and refrigerator. I ran to turn the circuit breaker off, saving his life. Another time, Brooke crawled under the kitchen cabinet and saw something shiny. She went to get it and it shocked her really bad. Bob discovered that someone had a wire to a bottle cap for a ground wire.

Things were certainly different in this country. It seemed that nothing worked properly and you couldn't get anything done in a day. Every little thing seemed to take so much time and effort. Truly Rome was not built in a day, and I could see why now.

Bob had been taking private language classes, but he was discouraged that he was not learning as fast as he thought he should so he told Mr. Morgan that he was going into town to the language school. Mr. Morgan decided to go as well and they learned at a much faster pace at the school in Naples. They would take the bus about 2:00 in the afternoon and would return about 7:30 p.m. It was winter and Bob would get so cold walking downtown to catch the bus back home. He would get hot chestnuts the peddlers on the side of the street would sell and put them in his pocket. He kept warmer on the way home with those hot chestnuts.

I had been doing a little better with the language, but I did make lots of mistakes like telling the clerk I wanted ten men instead of ten eggs and ordering dirt beef instead of ground beef. But one of the worst mistakes I made was with my neighbor. She had noticed how well behaved our children were and her child was a terror. She told me that her way of discipline was telling him that Jesus would come in the night and stick fire in his mouth if he was bad. She told him that the police were going to come take him away and he could never see them again. So she asked me what I did to control my children and I told her I spanked them with a wooden paddle or spoon. One day I saw her outside with her four year old chasing her with a plank. Later she told me she had tried to spank him with a plank but he got it from her and started spanking her. I gave up counseling.

There was a pasture in front of our house and I enjoyed seeing the shepherd come through with the sheep. One day the shepherds were leaning on the fence talking and not paying any attention and one of the little lambs got out in the road and was killed. It reminded me that our Good Shepherd never gets distracted and cares very attentively to his dear sheep. It was not long that another shepherd with another flock came by the same field. He was so careful with the sheep and would go before them and make sure that they were safe. One day he threw a snake over the fence into our yard to get it out of the sheep's way, because that would have scared them. God protects us the same way, even when we do not know it. And when it came time for Easter and they would have lamb to eat, the shepherd would hold the mother sheep in his lap and stroke her and try to soother her cries for her baby lamb. How much more does God care for us?

CHAPTER XIV

EARTH SHAKING

~:~

Luke 12:15 *Then he said to them, "Watch out! Be on
your guard against all kinds of greed; a man's life does
not consist in the abundance of his possessions."*

My parents planned a trip to come see us and I was so
excited that they were coming. It had been a year and
I did want to see them badly. I had missed them so much and
missed sharing what the children were doing. We planned
to show them much of the beauty of Italy. In preparation for
their arrival I had really worked very hard to get everything
perfect. They arrived on Friday so we drove to Rome to pick
them up. Mandy had hardly remembered them, and Brooke
did not even know who these people were. We all cried and
embraced.

A friend had told us of a place we could get great prices
on meat. Bob and gone and picked it up a week before they
arrived and I had put all the meat in the freezer. I thought it
smelled unusual, but did not think too much about it until I
thawed it out. The strange odor was there again. I got up early
on Sunday morning before anyone else and put the roast on
that we had purchased for our Sunday lunch. I wanted everything to be perfect since mom and dad were there.

We all got dressed and went to church. When we arrived home the entire house smelled of this awful odor. It was so bad I thought I was going to get sick. Needless to say we gave the roast to Elsa, our dog. We ended up going out for chicken. Bob and I determined that it must have been horse meat or worse since we had never encountered such a smell, although it was not spoiled.

The following day it hit again, my head was spinning just like it had before we left the States. Bob took me to the only English speaking doctor he could find at the International Hospital in Naples. The extremely old Swiss doctor decided I needed an internal. Stupid as I was, I let him do it. It had nothing to do with my head. I left disgusted and Bob took me to another doctor in Castel Volurno. The exam consisted of standing on one foot and closing my eyes. I fell to the side. He told me to stand on the other foot and I fell again. Yep! I was dizzy alright and he gave me medication for an ear infection. After a few days it went away, and we showed my parents some lovely sights including Pompeii and the Amalfi Drive on the coast line which was breath-taking.

Mother and dad were not all that impressed with Italy. My dad detested our being there at all. He didn't say too much, but some things he did say let me know that he thoroughly disapproved of us being missionaries and being in this backward country. I knew it bothered him to see us in such a financial strain, but we were not starving. God provided and we were pleased to be serving the Lord.

My dad and I had gone to the store to pick up some bread. When we returned we sat in the car a moment and he told me that he would pay for me and the children to come home. I was shocked at his words and was not for sure I heard him correctly. I started shaking with nervousness because I still had a fear of my father. I did not know what to say to him and said a silent prayer for help. He just could not grasp what this was all about. It was a sacrifice that we were willing to make to tell these people that God sent His only son for them and that whosoever believed in Him alone would have everlasting life with God in Heaven. (John 3:16) We knew what we were doing was not profitable at all; not on this earth anyway. We had nothing or anyone to depend on except the hand of God and we were pleased with how He was providing for us and how He met our every need. We knew we did not have as much as others, but we were there to do a job for the Lord. This was something that my parents just could not see or understand. They were looking from the outside of eternity and all they saw was their daughter and grandchildren without this world's material possessions and comforts of this life. My dad did not see the eternal value of us serving the Lord of Glory. This hurt me in so many ways. Why could not they see how much God had done for us? Why did they think Bob was a failure?

I told my dad, "No, I am not going to leave my husband. You just don't understand dad. I am happy serving the Lord, I know we don't have much, but it's not about having things. Dad, you just do not understand at all. I am happier than you have ever been." I did not tell Bob for several years about my conversation with my father. I knew it would not help their already strained relationship.

Another thing my parents did not understand about me was that I was a strong woman. I was strong not only spiritually, but also physically. When I knew something needed to be done, I did it. God gave me the strength to do things ordinary women could not do and I did things like carry water in five gallon jugs up twenty-five steps, move furniture, carry wood, build fires and what ever else I saw needed to be done. I was not one to sit and wait until someone else did it. My father failed to see that I was that much like him, and with my strong will he assumed that it was unfair for me to do so much.

A couple weeks after my parents returned to the states, Italy had a terrible earthquake. We were sitting in Church November twenty-third at 8:35 p.m. and the building began to shake. We all ran outside and tried to maintain our balance as the cars swayed back and forth. Being on the coast we were receiving the aftershocks which were like waves on the ocean. We later went home and the lights jingled all night as one aftershock after another hit. As the news unfolded the next day, there were thousands of people that went out into eternity in the disaster. About a month later we went to the epicenter to see the damage. Streets were still closed as the dead still remained under the rubble. Towns were totally leveled. The area looked like a war zone. We talked to many people and passed out tracts so they might find hope in Christ. Some were missing entire families. The hopelessness I saw on their faces haunted me for a long time.

The area was devastated. The people were distraught and grief stricken. Many people were homeless, so the government took over hotels, empty convents, schools and anything they could find to place the earthquake victims. Many people were relocated to our area in hotels. This gave us a wonderful opportunity to minister to these people.

The American Church had now called a new pastor from another work in Spain. Ted Woodruff and his family moved on the street behind our house. He was a fireball and funny at the same time. The American church was dissolved and a new one started. The name of the church was changed to Victory Baptist Church. Bob had been going to Naples to language school and had learned to speak very well, so he took Ted around and interpreted for him.

Early spring I was in bed with dizziness again. Only this time it lasted for eight days. But there was nothing to do. Nothing helped at all. I would get angry and cry, but the only thing that got me through was sleep. It was absolutely horrible. I questioned God, what had I done, why, what did

I need to learn, but no answers came. Finally like the times before, it subsided and I was back to normal although this was a very long episode. (For me normal was slightly dizzy all the time.)

Things were changing since Vince announced that he would no longer be coming to Naples each month. He thought that the time had come for us and the Morgans to start things on our own. We had a small group of people, but who would be their pastor? We had been working with the Morgans, but we knew that this would not work any longer. There must be a leader now that Vince was not coming back.

We had not always seen things eye to eye with the Morgans. For one thing, they had made comments to the Italians that if they would do certain things they might get saved. One time it was if a girl would stop wearing jeans she might get saved. Our conviction was that it did not matter what you had on, God looks on the heart. But we were stuck in this legalistic group of people. We heard messages on belt buckles, cowboy boots, ties, dresses, pants, and all the outward appearances. It disturbed us greatly, but we could do nothing but keep silent.

Morgan said he wanted to be the pastor of the work there in Naples so we began to look for an area where we could re-locate. There was no need for two missionaries to be in the same area when the gospel could be spread somewhere else. We looked and searched for somewhere to go, but after much prayer God did not seem to be opening anything up for us. For months we searched for a house to rent in some other town, but no one knew of anything. One day Mr. Morgan came to Bob and said that the Lord had revealed to him that he was the one that needed to move, not us. Within a month they were packed and Bob and Ted Woodruff helped move them to Sicily.

It was late spring that we were anxious to get a Bible Study started with a few people who had been saved under

Vince's ministry. They were faithful as long as we would pick them up to come. Then the thought occurred to us to start a Bible Club on Thursdays in the basement of the house. We had a large area that would accommodate a large crowd. We had some invitations printed and I took them around the neighborhood. One of the places we took invitations was a hotel where the earthquake victims lived. When we held our first meeting we had about twenty-five children from three years old to eighteen years old to come. We were thrilled and delighted that so many actually came.

They all giggled at first, I guess Bob murdered the language. We gave them cool- aid and cookies and they all played a while in our large yard. The next week thirty came then forty came and soon we had a steady crowd of fifty kids. Some of the mothers would come as well and listen as we would act out and tell them Bible stories. We were having as much fun as they were. It fascinated us when they would ask, "Is that really true?" Another would ask, "Did that really happen?" "Did Jesus really walk on the water?" "You mean the Bible says that a fish really swallowed Jonah?" Then they would tell us that some priest stuck his hand in the cleft and a whole mountain split. We had so many kids in the area because of the earthquake. And for months they would come and listen, until it got too cold and rainy then we opened up our home. One particular family came regularly. All eight of them came to our house for the Bible study. We were excited to see a man, Ciro, and his wife, Ernestina, come and bring their children.

We had been praying about renting a building and God opened the way. A building became available at the end of our street. There was much work to be done to it, and Ted Woodruff and Ciro helped build the necessary walls and bathrooms. The work was going slow but we were making good progress. Ciro worked everyday with Bob so he had the opportunity to witness to Ciro and to tell him of God's love. One day Ciro told Bob, "I've been watching you. I have been watching to see if what you are saying you are backing up with your life. I have tried to trick you into cheating and lying but I see what you have is real, and I want it also. Now, I believe all that you have told me about God is true, and I believe God's Word is true." Bob had the opportunity of leading Ciro to the Lord.

Bob was thrilled as he told me of Ciro's decision. I was excited too, although I was growing weary of their presence in our home every single day and night. They always showed up at supper and we would share what we had to eat with them. Ciro did not have a job, and we tried to pay him a little for helping Bob build the walls in the building but we did not have much ourselves. I loved to cook and we always seemed to have plenty to share. We knew the unemployment was about twenty-five percent in Italy but Ciro never seemed to be looking for a job. We would buy them some groceries now and then as we could afford it. We just felt so bad for them.

CHAPTER XV

CATHOLICISM

ᜀ᠄ᜀ

John 4:14 *"Whosoever drinketh of the water that I shall give him shall never thirst....a well of water springing up into everlasting life."*

We received a call in November from Bob's mother telling us his dad had been diagnosed with lung cancer. He had not smoked in thirty or more years. The kind of cancer he had more than likely came from exposure to asbestos. It was inoperable and fast growing. He had just retired and they were facing a very difficult time. It seemed so unfair. He had worked so hard all his life and now they were facing a scary, uncertain future. They were going to begin treatments but it was diagnosed as terminal.

Christmas of 1981 was unusually warm and we had the windows open as we had Christmas Dinner. Bob was not feeling too well and after Christmas he seemed to not be getting over whatever it was he had. Although he was not feeling well, he continued to work in the building eight to ten hours a day. I noticed he was eating like a horse but was losing weight. We dismissed it as we figured it was because he was working so hard. My suspicions grew when I also noticed him drinking and going to the bathroom constantly.

I called the states and had my parents to send test tapes for diabetes. When the test tapes came his sugar levels were so high they could not be measured. A blood test was the only way to find out how bad it was. He found a doctor and after a month of dieting his blood sugar was four hundred and fifty. They did not understand why he had not gone into a coma. It was only by the gracious hand of God on Bob that it was prevented. The doctor gave him some pills but he was highly allergic to them and itched so badly he almost went crazy. He stopped the pills and began a regiment of control through diet and exercise.

It was March and the weather was changing every day. Bob was feeling much better and was able to finish the work on the building. He had kept telling Ciro to find a job, because we had no more money to pay him, but he just hung around.

The church was in a good location for anyone to see. We were right on Via Dominciana, Via Apia, the road Paul himself walked up on his journey to Rome. This was now a four lane main highway that went up the west coast of Italy.

We had been praying for Ernestina for a long time. Ciro had made a profession of faith in the Lord, and we were wondering when she would follow suite. One morning she came to the house and asked if I would fix her hair. "Sure" I said. We went into the bathroom and I asked her to remove the earrings. I did not want to get the comb caught in her earrings since they were large gold loops. She turned to me and said. "Jane, why doesn't your church offer money for people to come like the Jehovah Witnesses do?"

"Well, Ernestina, for one thing we don't have the money." I continued. "You have been listening to Bob for a year now; you know you can't buy your way to heaven. You have to trust in Christ alone."

"You don't understand," she said. "It's okay for Ciro because he is a man but I can't get saved."

"What on earth are you talking about Ernestina?" I demanded.

"We aren't married. We are just living together and those aren't his kids either, only the last one." She seemed frustrated.

"That still does not matter; Ernestina, you and you alone need to trust the Lord." I said.

"I can't!" she said, decisively.

"Why?" I asked.

"Because, I am the bigger sinner. And God can't forgive me" she said in despair.

I took her to the kitchen and got my Bible in Italian and showed her the woman at the well in Luke. She read it aloud and was astonished at what the story was saying, and it spoke directly to her. She stopped and said "Oh! This is me, he is talking about me."

Then I asked her if she didn't want to receive Christ as her savior and she said she did. I took her to my bedroom and we both got down on our knees and she prayed. I prayed too, but silently I was praying for her to receive Christ as her savior. After she prayed she stood up and said. "He is gone! The devil is gone. He sat right here on my shoulder and told me I couldn't get saved that I was too big of a sinner. I feel so light I could fly. The burden is gone!"

We both cried and she wanted to go tell Bob and Ciro. When we returned to my house she seemed concerned for her earrings. I assured her that they were where she left them, but she said, "No, you don't understand. I wore that little horn on the earring on the same side the devil sat on my shoulder and told me I could not get saved. I have to get rid of that thing. A witch gave it to me and said if I wore it on my right earring I would have good luck."

I was astonished to hear such a thing. She continued. "If I had not taken that off I might not have ever gotten saved. The devil kept telling me not to listen to Bob."

Ernestina really changed and wanted to tell everyone about her newly found faith in Christ. We went on visitation and she was the one who witnessed and answered questions. If anyone said, I heard that you don't believe in Mary, she would say, yes we do, she is the mother of Jesus. It was amazing to hear her witness for Christ.

Our little meetings were growing; we had about twenty in attendance now. Not all were believers yet, but God was working and they had a lot of questions. They were slow to trust anyone since they saw the lies the priest told. The priest also threatened the people and children that were coming to our Bible study. They told them that if they came eternal life would be taken from them; they would have to stay in purgatory forever. They also threatened the parents and told them if they came they would lose their jobs. The majority of the people stayed with us. One gentleman really hated the Catholic Church. We listened intently as he told us about his son that had been killed in a motorcycle wreck a few years before. He said "The Catholic Church is like a big super store. Everything you need and do costs you money. When you are born, they want money to christen you, when you are twelve years old it costs to have you confirmed into the church, your first communion costs, to get married costs, it costs when you have children and when you die, it costs to pray you out of purgatory."

That summer we would sit on our porch and watch the house across the canal being robbed several times. We knew some Americans lived there. One night I called the police as they were robbing the place and they could have caught them had they come immediately. They showed up two hours later. Our watchman also was found murdered under a bridge right after that. We never found out any details of the murder. We were beginning to feel like it was not the safest place to be so we started looking for another house in a safer area. House number nine, here we come.

We had about eleven that were going to be baptized in April. We were planning a big luncheon after the baptism. Then we found out that the President of the Bible College we attended was in the country and wanted to come down to see us. We felt so honored that they would want to visit us. It was always exciting to have visitors from the states and we wanted to show them the area. We had arranged the baptism so as not to interfere with the Tates visit, but their schedule was changed and they would be coming the weekend that we planned the baptism. We did not want to disappoint the Italians so we continued with our plans to have the baptism although the Tates would be there.

The President and his wife came in on Saturday morning. We explained that we had not planned to be busy with the work, but to be hospitable to them. But they seemed pleased that we were doing a baptism. We took them to see Naples and Pompeii on Saturday afternoon. We got stuck in traffic in Naples and sat for hours. The Tates were getting very nervous and inquired if it was a normal occurrence for the police to stand on the street corners with their fingers on the triggers of the machine guns. It was something we had to gotten used to ourselves. Naples was a violent city. Crime was everywhere. One day when we were down in the heart of Naples a car drove up and fired into another car with machine guns killing five people, and drove off. When we first arrived in Naples we had heard of a thief who ripped a gold chain off a child and cut his juggler vein and the child died. So we were used to hearing about all the crime.

As we gathered on the beach on Sunday afternoon about fifty people attended the baptism. Others gathered around asking questions. Still others watched from a distance as Bob baptized Ernestina, Ciro, and others one by one in the cold waters of the Mediterranean that crisp spring day. Later Bob admitted that the water was much colder than he expected, but no one complained and we had a glorious time of celebration as we returned to our house for a fellowship meal.

As summer approached there were a lot of things on our hearts when Bob's brother called and told us that his dad had almost died but he was okay for now. He told us if we wanted to see him we needed to come home sometime very soon. Ernestina and Ciro were not getting along too well either, then the dollar dropped and our financial situation was getting critical. We knew that it was time to go home so we could raise the support we needed to remain in Italy.

For the time being Ernestina and Ciro were our biggest concerns. They were fussing about money problems all the time. We could never figure out where they got the money they needed for food, and he always had money for cigarettes and gas. One afternoon they came by the house while Bob and the girls were not there. They started a real big fuss and then broke out into a fight. Then Ernestina said something that really upset Ciro. He became very irate and grabbed Ernestina around her throat and started choking her. She was screaming for the police and saying someone call the police. She got away from him but he caught her and started choking her again. I was terrified and did not know what to do. Could I stand there and watch him kill her and I thought that was what he was going to do. I instinctively grabbed the broom near by and hit Ciro as hard as I could over the head. I don't even remember thinking about what I was doing. It stopped him cold and broke my broom too. Then he came at me and said, "Do you know what you have done?" Twice he repeated himself. All I could think of was, "If you touch me Bob will kill you." He looked at me funny like he did not understand. I was so frightened that my English came out and I repeated myself in Italian.

He left in a hurry leaving Ernestina with me crying. Bob came home a short time later and I told him that I hit Ciro in the head with a broom. He said, "You what?!!!"

We talked the situation over and Ernestina said she was going to leave him anyway. We took her home later and Ciro met us outside. He started pushing Bob around, threatening to kill him, and said he had a gun. Bob told him to load his gun that we were not going anywhere. This was the biggest mess we had ever encountered and did not know that people actually acted like this. We spent several sleepless nights in prayer and wondering how all this confusion was going to end up. We had already booked our flight back home and really did not want to leave this mess in the hands of our successor.

Church services continued and one by one they all came back. Ciro even came back. We learned that Italians in general like a big show. Their bark is loud but they are pretty much harmless. Twice we had been threatened, and it really did not feel very good. But Paul himself was beaten, threatened and thrown in jail. We had never suffered as much as Paul. We were not martyred for Christ.

When our replacement came we had to tell him to be understanding with these folks. For the most part they were not saved or were very new Christians and were very immature yet. We asked him to continue with the youth program. To reach a society that is unsaved you have to start teaching young people the truth of God's Word.

On this first term in Italy we learned much about Roman Catholicism. We had known some things before, but we had been exposed first hand to some earth shattering doctrines that the Roman Catholic people in the United States do not know about. Most Catholic people do not know what the Catholic Church teaches about their beliefs. I am a firm believer in the Scripture and God's Word is the ultimate and only authority. Commentaries are good, but we do not need any other book or idea to take precedence over the Bible. There are a lot of denominations that have another authority other than God's Word and we must realize that Jesus said,

"I am the Way, the Truth and the Life, no man comes to the Father except through Me." There is no other way, no other man, no other set of rules, no other avenue or values and no traditions whereby you can obtain eternal life. Christ is the only way.

So when we visited the empty churches in Italy and talked with the people, we understood their frustration with the Catholic Church. We had folks tell us all kinds of tales that went on with their priest, all sorts of tales that we heard about the nuns, weird and bazaar stories about the Church. It was no wonder that the people in Italy lost all hope in their religion. It reminds me of a story that I heard about a man walking down a long country road carrying a heavy bundle on his back. Someone came along side him on a wagon and offered him a ride, so he hopped on the back of the wagon but failed to put the bundle down. Religion is the same way; it will take you for the ride, but it will not remove the burden. Ultimately, religion has no real eternal value. We saw people everywhere in Italy that were so religious, more so than people in America. They prayed often, they would bow down to statues, they would have the priest come and bless their homes, take communion, go to confession, light candles, say their rosary, say their Hail Mary's, at one of the festivals they would cut themselves and crawl on broken glass so they would have forgiveness of their sins, walk up a staircase in a church and chant prayers for forgiveness of sin, kiss statues, pray to Mary and numerous other things, but they did not have the peace of God in their hearts. They did not have the forgiveness of sin that removed their burden.

The Roman Catholic Church had lied to the people and preyed upon their ignorance for centuries. They teach them that salvation is in the Catholic Church alone. They told them they could not have a bible or read it that only the church could interpret the Bible. They invented a place called purgatory, so the church could profit and the people would have to pay money to get out of a place that did not even exist. They obliterated one of the commandments that says "Thou shalt have no other gods before me. Thou shalt not make unto thee any carved images....thou shalt not bow down to them." Then they split another commandment into two commandments so there would still be ten. They taught that infant baptism is essential in the removal of original sin. Only the priest drinks the wine at communion so it will not get spilled and the people take the wafer, but it actually turns into the body and blood of Christ when you swallow it.

One of their doctrines is that Mary is co-mediator and co-redeemer with Christ. She answers prayers, and she was conceived sinless just like Christ. A lot of people I have talked to say, well I am catholic but I don't believe that way. But that is what the Catholic Church in Rome teaches. That is their roots of belief. That is why I am not associated with the Catholic Church. I am not associated with any other teachings other than what is founded upon scripture alone. We do not need to follow some man's opinion or some traditional ideas. We need only to follow Christ and that is a narrow way.

There is one church in the Naples area called Saint Gennaro that was founded on the tradition that a priest was beheaded and his head rolled down hill and landed on this spot where they built a church. Every year they have a celebration to determine if there will be blessing or curse for Italy. They have a vial of blood in which they say is the actual blood of this Saint. The priest will pray and chant for hours if needed to see if the blood will liquefy and again bring good luck for Italy for another year. Sometimes it does literally turn into liquid form, I saw it one time on a special TV program. But Satan has great power to fool a society that is superstitious with a supernatural event. One year that it did not liquefy was in 1981, and that was the year of the terrible earthquake.

Still others would run to see a statue bleed or cry real tears. The heartbreak of religion is that it has only an empty hope. I thank God daily that I am not in the darkness of religion, but in the Light of Jesus Christ.

CHAPTER XVI

THE HOME GOING

꒰ :꒱

John 11:25 *I am the resurrection and the life; he that believeth in me, though he were dead, yet shall he live,*

R oss and Sarah had become good friends as we often visited each other. They had become family as we spent holidays and vacation time with each other. Some times Ross would come to Naples and preach for Bob, and we would have a good time together. Their children were like big brother and sister to Mandy and Brooke. They played together although they were some older. And now as we were returning to the States in August 1982, for a few months, we would stay with them overnight and they would take us to the airport the next morning.

As we drove off to go to the airport, I gazed at Elsa, our boxer. Tears started streaming down my face. I felt like we were abandoning her. She had been such a great companion and protector for three years. Somehow I knew I would never see her again.

The drive really wasn't too long, just 3 hours. The next morning we got up very early and Ross took us to the airport at 8:00 a.m. Bob had found a good deal on tickets and we were going to fly a Charter Plane. It cost about sixteen hundred dollars round trip for all four of us. We had given Ross all our Italian currency since we would be boarding the plane shortly and had no need of it, or so we thought. After entering the airport and finding our boarding gate we waited and waited, but the flight was coming in from England and had not landed yet. We had only toast for breakfast and the children were getting hungry. We were supposed to board the plane at 10:00 a.m. but now it was lunch time. At last the plane arrived and we were allowed to board at 1:30 p.m., however, they announced that there would be no food served because we were going to land in Milan in one hour and there would not be enough time to eat. We sat in Milan for hours as they were checking each ticket. They had too many passengers and were short one seat. The flight had been over-booked. They were particularly interested in Brooke's ticket, since she was so young, but we had paid for her seat. After about an hour of searching for a seat an announcement was made that someone would have to stay behind. One little old lady was crying, she wanted to go home, but my kids were crying too because they had not eat all day. Someone finally stayed behind so the plane took off at 7:00 p.m.

The children settled down after they ate to watch the movie. They were so exhausted, we all were. Flying made me so nervous I could not relax. The girls were excited so they did not go to sleep until an hour or two before we landed in New York. Everything they saw was strange to them. Brooke was overwhelmed with the airport, how big the plane was (airport hallway), and water in the commode. After we went through customs we had to reach my parents to let them know that they should not leave for the airport in Greensboro. We had missed our connecting flight. The airlines would put us up in a hotel for the night. By the time we got to a room and ordered supper it was 11:00 p.m. and we were drained. The girls were excited and wanted to eat supper since their bodies were on a different time clock. We slept for about four hours then had to get ready for the morning flight.

Tears filled my eyes often on the plane as I thought about seeing everyone at home. I was getting so emotional maybe because I was so tired. As we were approaching the airport I was getting the girls cleaned up some and Brooke looked and me and asked if Me Maw and Papaw were American like us or if they were Italian. She did not remember when my parents came over; they were going to be strangers to her as well as Bob's parents.

We spotted our families waiting and we ran to greet them. We were all chatting, laughing, hugging and crying. Bob's mother came over to me and said. "Come see Paw." In all the excitement I had over looked him. The kindest, loving, sweetest father-in-law any girl could ever have, and I forgot him. How could I have overlooked him, I was his favorite daughter-in law? My heart sank as I approached this frail, glassy eyed man sitting in a wheelchair. I hugged and kissed him but it was like he was not there, he said very little. He looked ninety years old instead of sixty-six. His hair was all gone along with the rest of his personality. Cancer treatment had left this wonderful man a mere weak and lifeless body.

We lived with my parents for about two months. It was tight in their small two bedroom house, but the girls really did not mind sleeping on the pull out couch in the living room. They thought it was a big party every night. We tried to unpack as best as we could but knew that we needed to find a place to live and knew that we could probably move back into the church house.

By the first of November we had everything arranged with the church and moved into the beige house beside the Church again. (This had been our eleventh move in our seven years of marriage.) Our support had been dropping for a long time so Bob was considering leaving the mission board. It was because of them that we were losing support. They had done some things that were not quite appropriate for the ministry. We prayed and made some plans and were led to start our own mission board through our church. We were going to be the only missionaries with Italian Baptist Ministries but we had to set it up like a board for tax purposes. Bob wrote a letter to all our churches that supported us and told them what we were doing and how we could still receive the funds.

We contacted our mission board and also sent them a letter of resignation. They had great indignation toward us and told us that they would contact all our supporters. They did and lied to them. Accusations were made that we came home without permission from the board. Through their lies and deceit we lost our support for that month of November. We had seven hundred dollars coming to us but they kept it and said we owed it to them. The board said that the van we bought in Italy was theirs; that it belonged to them. We paid for the van ourselves out of our escrow account however, the president of the board thought everything we had belonged to the mission board.

We had no money. I don't remember how we made it that month and the months ahead, but somehow through God's provision and grace we survived. We had justification to take the Mission Board to court and get our support they kept. What kind of Christian would do this to missionaries? Bob said that he could not take them to court. We would have to put it out of our minds and hearts. We had to forgive and go on.

Friends, family and churches knew our dilemma and would say, "If we can do anything to help in any way just let us know." Our needs were pretty much visible, how could they not know? We were not going to ask anyone to help. We would leave it up to God; He already knew who would have an open heart. Often when people make a statement like that they just want off the hook. But God supplied our needs through those who had a willing heart to listen to Him and obey his word.

So many times we all forget that if we see our brother in a need and we have it in our possession then we are commanded to help. How can the love of God be in us if we take no pity on those who are in need? "This then is how we know that we belong to the truth, and how we set our hearts at rest in his presence." I John 3:16-19. We are to love our brothers enough to lay our lives down for them.

Our problems became our focus and we forgot how bad Bob's dad had been. Shortly, he was taken to the hospital and was admitted to the ICU unit. It did not appear to be good at all. The chemotherapy and cobalt treatments had destroyed the lung tissue and the lungs were no longer capable of supplying the oxygen to the blood stream. However, the immediate problem was that they had given him so much glucose and he had gone into a diabetic comma. He was not eating and had been so weak.

Bob was staying by his father's side day and night. I went when I could manage to get away from the children, but I had problems with my dizziness again. My focus never really got better after that, I felt like I was in a fog all the time. Paw had regained consciousness and we thought that he might pull through for a short time. But within twenty-four hours he was back in a coma. His brain was not receiving proper oxygen and brain cells were dying. While Bob and his mother were holding Paws hand, he slipped into the arms of the angles and they carried him into the presence of God during the night, November eighteenth.

Ruth, Bob's mother, reached over and kissed Paw on the head, patted his hands and said, "I'll see you in a little while." That was the vivid picture I remember at the funeral home on visitation night. People were visiting from miles around. Paw was a very good man and would be greatly missed. My parents drove over and paid their respects to Bob's family. I remember how bad I thought my dad looked that night. He said nothing and acted like he was so tired.

"Because He Lives, I Can Face Tomorrow", was sung at the funeral. It was Paw's very favorite song and he lived every word of that song. Afterward, I noticed that my mother and my sister came to the funeral and asked, "Mom, where is daddy?"

"Well, he wasn't feeling well, Jane." She said sweetly.

"Okay, well, I guess we will see you later, I think we might stay here a few days with Bob's mother." I replied.

We followed the funeral procession to the grave yard. The grave side services were short that cold November day. When we got back to Ruth's house, my mother called and said that my dad had a heart-attack. We rushed to Winston-Salem to the hospital where he had been admitted to ICU. I was frightened that I might lose my dad also. Soon the doctor let us know that the prognosis was good and that he would recover.

It took some time for him to recover. My mother was still working and wanted to know if I or my sister would come stay with him during the day. I had the kids to take care of but I could have arranged for someone to help out with that, but I was so afraid he would have another heart-attack and I would not know how to handle it. A couple months after my dad recovered, he took an early retirement. He bought a motor home with the retirement bonus and was planning a future of relaxation and travel. But he was working harder than ever. He built a shed for his motor home which was quite a big job.

In February we took Bob's mother to Florida with us. It was nice to get away and try to enjoy the children at Disney World. On our way back home we stopped in Charleston, SC to see Bob's grandmother. She was eighty-nine and did not have long to live. She had a stroke which left her in a coma.

We left Bob's mother there to help care for her and a couple weeks later she passed away.

We had been traveling trying to see our supporting churches and trying to raise some more support. Our trip home had cost us tremendously in more ways that we cared for. Our support level was about three hundred dollars a month and we were sending that to Italy for the rent on the house. We were very frustrated. This was supposed to be an enjoyable trip home, visiting churches and seeing family and friends. We had planned only to be in the States for six months and the time was up. How could we go back to Italy under supported again? We just couldn't. We had so many mixed emotions and so many questions on every hand. Some were asking us, "Why do you need to go back, why don't you just settle down a get a job like a normal person, let someone else go?" Sounded like good excuses but we just could not rest. We were exhausted emotionally and in every other way, but we were still so burdened for the Italian people and wanted them to know the truth that could set them free from sin.

It hit me again; I got so dizzy I was sick to my stomach. I could not lift my head off the pillow. The preacher and elders came and laid hands on me and prayed for this illness to leave. The next day I was some better and again it took me a few days to regain my pace. The dizziness always made me angry. I would often cry because I wanted to be in control and this is one thing I could have no control over. I felt helpless and powerless when I would get these spells.

We continued to travel and slowly we began to pick up a little support. There were great pastors and there were bad pastors. They all were men who were just like everyone else. Some would tell you anything to get you out of their hair. A few told us that we would be hearing from them soon, and never hear anything. Several told us that they would call us next week and let us know what the church decided and we never heard a word. Some were very gracious and did exactly as they said they would do. By June our support level raised to about eight hundred dollars a month and we could get some of our bills paid.

Then the news broke. Italy was putting all missionaries out of the country ASAP if they did not have their visa. No one else would be allowed back into the country without a Visa. That had been the law in Italy but had never been enforced, at least not until now. There were a lot of laws for that matter, but for the most part they ignored them. Bob called the consulate, but they told us to call back in a year or two and they would see about our visa then. That did not sound like what we wanted to hear. What was God doing? Did he not want us back in Italy as soon as we could get there? There were people who needed to hear the message of salvation why could we not get back now?

Again, we were faced with questions and could not understand what was happening. One of the biggest questions was, did God want us back? Why did we have so much trouble getting back? First we lost almost all of our support, now this. Once again God reminded me that He was in control and to trust in Him. That had been so hard for me.

Decisions are not easy to make and this was difficult. "What do we do now, Lord? Do we tell the churches we can't get back right now? Do we continue to raise support?" Our hearts sank deep. What were we going to do? We had no money for a lawyer to fight our way into the country and no one to pull strings and get us back in. We knew some baptist missionaries like Ross and Sarah that could stay because they had a residence permit and some others were forced out of the country.

Weeks dragged by, and we talked and prayed and planned what we could and should do next. We analyzed our situation and our experience. We were tired of deputation and tired of dragging the children all over the country, from one church to another, week after week, and spending all our income on travel. Being discouraged about deputation did not help us in making the right decision, but we made one. And we did not know at the time if we were doing what God wanted us to do, but we felt it was right. All we wanted to do was to do what God wanted us to do and we did not know exactly what that was. Looking back, God had put a peace in our hearts and we felt that we should ask the churches to stop our support since we could not tell then when we would return. We were sensitive about the church's money and did not want to take the money dishonestly. We knew other missionaries who stayed in the states for years and continued taking support and that bothered us.

Bob had to return to Italy and close out our house, so we waited until his return to tell our churches. He sold everything we had taken over, except a few pictures, some towels and my china we stored at Ross and Sarah's house in Rome, and one vase I made him promise to bring home. He got a job in a furniture store and enrolled in graduate school to work on a Master in Counseling. Our plan was to return to Italy with a job and some support. We could obtain a work visa which was nothing to get, and Bob could teach in college there. The idea of "tent making missionaries" came from one of the books he was reading which sounded great to us. The term refers to someone who considers himself as a missionary but takes a job in the country he wants to enter.

My dad had another heart attack through the summer and had open heart surgery while Bob was away in Italy. He came through the surgery quite well, but it took a while for recovery again. Time dragged by and everything seemed mundane after that. We struggled constantly financially. Bob was hardly bringing home enough money for us to survive. There was no time for us anymore with him working and going to school. We did not get to see each other except when Bob was dead tired or studying. We had been living in a mobile home we purchased before Bob went to Italy to close everything out there. Since we were no longer considered missionaries we knew we had to vacate the church house. But the church was gracious to let us put the mobile home on the same property that we were on when Mandy was born. Some time later we moved that mobile home to a trailer lot in hopes that when we returned to Italy we could sell it easier.

After a year we became restless and were anxious to return to Italy. Bob had about twenty-four more hours left to take in classes to finish his master's degree. We called on a few churches and told them of our desire to return and that we felt that we could be ready in about a year. That would be when Bob would finish his Masters degree. Several of the churches picked up our support immediately. We continued to use the mission board we had created and a very bright young man in our church oversaw all the income and disbursements.

As time permitted we began the road to deputation again. We visited churches and made calls and began to feel that it would not take us as long to raise our support this time. The girls did so well with the idea of going back, especially Amanda. They did not particularly enjoy singing, but they were so cute with their little missionary song. The people in the churches really enjoyed their song and always complemented us on how well behaved the girls were and how sweet they seemed.

Missionary Kids Song

My life is far from normal it's as weird as it can be,
And if you compare me with your child, I think that you
    would agree.
I can talk a funny language, and I never know where's
    home,
And Next time I wake up, I could be half way to Rome.

I'm a missionary's kid, and sometimes, it makes me
 sad,
When I travel all the time or I have to be without my
 dad.
But no matter what you say it's the price I'm called to
 pay
And my Jesus will reward me up in heaven some day.

As long as I'm an MK I must be a perfect child,
Oh but for a moment just to scream and go run wild.
Now don't run around, just sit still and be careful what
 you say,
Next time I'm in church I'm going to ask the preacher
 for my pay!

I'm a missionary's kid, and sometimes, it makes me
 sad,
When I travel all the time or I have to be without my
 dad.
But no matter what you say it's the price I'm called to
 pay
And my Jesus will reward me up in heaven some day.

It was the middle of October 1985 and Bob was getting
ready for work. The phone rang and it was surprising to hear
the voice of a man in Ohio who supported us a few years
previously. He owned a large company that made football
covers. He wanted to know how much more support we
needed before we could leave for the mission field. When
Bob got off the phone he could not contain himself. He was
so excited as he shared with me that this company might
pick-up the rest of our support needed to return. He said he
could finish his Master through correspondence. I was not
too sure about all I was hearing. Sure enough in November
he called back and asked how soon we could leave. I was not

ready to leave that day and it sounded like he wanted us to leave pretty soon. There was a lot to think about and to do. The children were not prepared for this change so rapidly either. And it might take us a while to sell the mobile home.

We could not believe how fast God was moving. Bob finished the fall semester while we made calls and plans. God had provided the means for us to return but how would we get back into the country? Bob called the Italian Consulate in Washington to inquire about our visa. Within a few hours they called back and said, "Here it is, we found it. Your visa has been approved." We were astounded at how God was working all the details in order for us to return. Surely this is of the Lord! We felt like we had the stamp of approval to make plans to leave immediately.

Christmas flew by so fast and nothing was dull any longer. Our flight was booked for February 14, 1986 and my head was spinning again. Why did it have to hit me at the most inconvenient times? Of course my mother blamed it on my nerves and life style. Only this time, I began to treat myself with some sinus medication, which helped. It did not seem to last as long. Then I began to notice that if I ate salty things it was worse. I had been to an ear, nose and throat doctor and she could not pinpoint it, but it sounded like Mieniers disease. The sinus medication seemed to dry out the fluid build up in the balancing part of my inner ear. It did not take care of the problem fully and I really had to watch what I ate and stress seemed to effect it as well. But after about nine years of this dizziness I was getting some knowledge of what was going on.

Through an ad in the paper we found someone to take over payments on the mobile home, but we had to leave it in our name and the payments came out of our account. We had told the couple that the agreement would be, if they defaulted in any way the mobile home would come back to us and they would lose all monies invested. We were careful to make sure all the paper work was notarized properly and that they fully understood all the terms and conditions of the contract.

Packing and shipping things we needed was exciting to say the least. The girls were understanding and did not complain that they had to give up their things to go back to Italy. We had been home a little over two years and they had forgotten much about being there, but Amanda remembered much more since she was older and did not mind returning. Brooke was a little more reluctant about leaving her friends behind. Of course my parents did not want us to return and especially my mom could not understand why we wanted to go back. Dad just did not say much, he had been much quieter since his open-heart surgery. But soon everything was done and we spent a week with my folks and then a few days with Bob's mom before we left. This time when we went to the airport only a few friends and family went to see us off. We said our goodbyes and boarded the plane with tears once again streaming. There was so much to think about on our trip back to Rome.

CHAPTER XVII

MY HEART'S DESIRE

⌣∶⌣

Psalms 37:4 *Delight thyself also in the Lord and he shall give thee the desires of thine heart.*

Bob joked about this being the best Valentine's present any girl could ask for, a trip to Rome, Italy. He still tells people he took me to Rome one Valentine's since we left on February 14, 1986. We landed and Ross and Sarah were excited to see us at the airport. I was real concerned about Mandy being so sick. She had been to the doctor the day we left. She almost had pneumonia and Ross and Sarah's house was so very cold, I was afraid she would become worse. They did have one room that they heated with a wood stove. Soon Mandy recovered and I was thankful.

We had a lot to catch up on with the Stumps and we always enjoyed being with them. Sarah made sure that we were welcomed and could stay as long as we needed. It was great to see everyone and how much their children had grown. Since it was so cold we especially enjoyed fixing pizza in the wood stove. Ross had a steel grill that fit into the wood stove and actually cooked the pizza over the coals. It made the best pizza anywhere. We would eat and talk for many hours.

Renato, a young man across the street from the Stumps was always a joy to see. He played the guitar quite well and had written some new songs. He had accepted the Lord under Ross's ministry some years earlier and was growing in the Lord by leaps and bounds. Ross took him under his wing and taught him as much as anyone could get in a bible college. He also was a very studious young man like none you had ever seen before. God was preparing him for a special ministry in Italy.

Upon returning we had been praying and asked the Lord where would he have us to go. Someone else had already taken the work in Naples and we did not want to intrude upon their ministry. We felt a great desire to go to a place called Gaeta. It was a town between Naples and Rome on the coast. There was a military port there where American ships came in and would often stay for a month or more. Some of the sailors would have their families with them. We visited that city on occasion when we lived in the Naples area and found that there were no missionaries working in that area. We knew that the people in the Naples area were very southern, hospitable, and receptive to the gospel. Not knowing many people in Gaeta, we did not know if they would be receptive. The only one person we knew was an Italian lady married to an American. She had come down to our church as often as she could make it in Castel Volturno. She was a young Christian and enjoyed the services in her language although she spoke English very well.

The train ride to Gaeta was always nice, although we had to leave Rome extremely early to have a full day looking for an apartment. Ross always accompanied us and sometimes I would not go at all. It took us several trips and time after time we were told that there were no apartments available for rent. Every time we went to a realtor Bob and Ross spoke Italian. One time we came out again discouraged that there was nothing available. I asked them to go back in and ask if there was any place to rent to an American. "Yes!" Indeed there was. That was all it took, because the Italians do not want to rent to the Italians. There are not enough homes in Italy for everybody, and when an Italian gets a place you can not get them out. Often times these people would build a home for their children for the future and rent them out to Americans. It is a wise idea they had. By renting them out to the Americans, we would pay for them, and then when their children would get married they would have a house for them that was paid for. They would mostly rent to the military.

Sarah was saddened that we had found a place and would be leaving so soon. I don't know why, because we spent a month with them. Their house was extremely large, probably four thousand square foot. No one got into anyone else's way and everyone got along great. We did our part and bought groceries, and anything else we felt was needed. I enjoyed our stay but it was time to leave. Bob left very early that morning to pick up some things we would need. He rented a truck and picked up some bed frames, mattresses, a stove and refrigerator. That was all we needed for the time being. The apartment was tiny with two bedrooms. It was fairly new and was real nice. It was quite a change from Ross and Sarah's large house.

The girls and I left later that morning. We took the bus and then the subway to the train station. The subway was so packed I could not move an inch. We had to stand up all the way to central down town to the train station. The girls and I boarded the train about 10:00 a.m. for Gaeta. I was so loaded down with baggage I was afraid I would loose sight of the girls, especially Brooke. I told them to hold on tight to me until we could find a seat. The train ride was exciting for the girls; it had been a very long time since they had ridden a train. We pulled up to the station in Gaeta and unloaded. Bob was waiting on us with the truck and we drove to the apartment. We unloaded the truck and took it back. We would have to walk back to the apartment but that wasn't too bad.

Somewhere I found out that mine and the girls' passports were missing as well as my entire billfold along with my credit cards and check book. I had been pick-pocketed on the subway; that must have been where it happened. It was so crowded I could not tell if someone brushed against me and pulled it out of my purse. We had to get to a phone and call somebody back in the states to have our credit card cancelled. We did not have a phone yet. It was getting dark and the only phone we knew of was on the other side of town about two miles away. We left the girls alone, for the first time in their lives so we could trek across town to use the phone. I cried almost all the way, I did not want the girls to have to be alone in a strange house, with no way to get in touch with anyone and they could not even speak the language. God, why is all this happening? And my faith began to grow weak as I took my eyes off the Lord. But things have a way of working out and soon I forgot the pain of that experience.

I was so excited because I could help Bob in the ministry now that Amanda and Brooke were old enough to stay some on their own. Amanda was going to be nine in June and Brooke seven in April. I had it all planned out in my mind how I was going to visit the ladies and learn some more of the Italian language. Maybe some day soon I could even have a ladies bible study. I had sat in on an Italian class at the School of the Arts the fall before we left and had learned right much more of the language. I knew I was no where as good as the Stumps or even close to being good enough yet to do anything.

In March and April we were busy getting furniture and getting settled. It was so pleasant to be fully supported and have enough money to get the things we needed. We found the couple that we had known from the area and met up with them. We got together on several occasions and had a few meals with them. She was excited to see that we were back and wanted to help us in the ministry. They had a darling little blond headed boy about two years old. I loved children so much and held him as often as he would sit on my lap. I even commented that if I could have another child, I would want one like him. He was so sweet. (I didn't know that God was listening.)

We had taken the girls to the school to see if we could get them enrolled and they told us to forget it. They had no room for outsiders and their rooms were packed, and besides they had not mastered the language, how would they understand anything? We grew to appreciate what we had left behind in the States. It took a couple phone calls but we got in touch with Ted Woodruff. He had moved to San Vito, about nine hours of driving time away. He sent us the papers, so we could test the girls and get them set up for fall on a home schooling program that was designed for teaching missionary children on the field. Since the Italians in Gaeta would not let them attend we had to school them ourselves. They did very well on their test. Taking them out of school in February did not affect them at all and they were right on grade level.

Mid-April I started getting sick and did not feel well at all. I was so tired all the time. Bob was tired of me complaining and laying around so much. By the end of the month I could not even go grocery shopping. Walking about one block would wear me out and I was so exhausted I could go no further. I got my medical book out and was sure that I had cancer. I also lost my appetite. This really worried me. I could not stand the taste of meat which is a typical symptom of stomach cancer according to my medical book. I told Bob of my concern and I know that he was agitated with me. He told me to go back to the states if I wanted to so I could see a doctor. He did not think I had cancer. But something was really wrong.

Talking with my neighbor one day I explained all my symptoms and she said I had Spring Fever. I knew it was not a case of laziness but this was something else. A week later I asked her again if she knew of a doctor I could call, and explained to her that I was feeling worse and it was not Spring Fever. She came down to my apartment at 9:00 p.m. and said that the doctor was on his way. I was not aware that they made house calls.

My house was a wreck and I did not look much better. The doctor came promptly at 10:00 p.m. and started asking questions. We talked about my bout with diarrhea that lasted for eleven days. Then the sickness started with nausea. Maybe it was a virus that has lasted a month. "No" he said. He took me and Bob to the bedroom and I lay on the bed while he mashed on my stomach. After a few more questions he said. "I think you are pregnant."

"Oh, no, that can't be possible. I had a tubule ligation in America seven years ago." I said.

"Well, they have been known to grown back you know." He responded.

I could not believe what I was hearing. But I knew that it could not be possible. He gave me some vitamins and said I was probably anemic. After he left we just laughed that he thought I was pregnant. The vitamins did the trick and I was better in one week. But the doctor insisted that I be seen by a gynecologist in the area. I was feeling so much better and did not want to go, but Bob suggested that I go anyway. He stayed with the girls and the neighbors upstairs, both her and her husband took me to the gynecologist. I did not speak that well in Italian but we managed to communicate. I was terribly embarrassed with the questions the doctor was asking in front of my neighbors who were trying to help with the language difficulty. He asked me to go into the examining room. There was no nurse, only him and me. He pulled off his gloves after the examination and said, "Signora, tu sei due mese ingravidanza." (Lady, you are two months pregnant.) Well, I set him strait,

"No I'm not!"

"Oh, yes you are!" And proceeded to tell me how he knew. I told him I did not believe him, and asked if he could do a urine test. He said I was wasting my money. I walked out with my mouth hung open in unbelief.

When I arrived home, Bob met me and the neighbors at the door. I was crying and the neighbors were beaming with joy as they announced to Bob that I was pregnant. I thought his jaw would hit the floor like mine almost did. They left and he followed me to the balcony where I was bawling. I did not want the girls to see how upset I was. We talked for awhile. I do not know what I was at that moment; all I knew was that I was not happy. I had plans and it did not include a baby and being tied down to another child. I was going to help Bob in the ministry. I was going to pass out tracts and go door to door, and have ladies bible studies. How could God allow this to happen to me, and why now? As we told the girls they were relieved that I was not going to die, but they did not want a baby either, especially Brooke. She had been the baby and she let it be known that she did not want a baby in our family, because she would not be the baby anymore.

It was difficult to know what to do at this point. I had to find a doctor that I could trust and a hospital that knew what they were doing. This would be my third C-Section and I could not just trust anybody to do it. We made a visit to Rome so we could tell Ross and Sarah the not so good news. She suggested that I make an appointment with the doctor that was the gynecologist for all the high ranking military wives in Rome. I got an appointment for a month away which would put me at four months. Sarah said that he would probably be good. I trusted her judgment and I had no other ideas.

All I could do for the next four weeks was to swing in the swing and complain and cry that I did not want another child. Frankly, I was angry with God. I felt like this had messed up my life. Like, Elijah, who sat under the juniper tree, I was thinking, poor me. We did not even know anyone who had three children. What would we do with this child? There was no room in the house for another bed. My perspective was pretty messed up. We didn't have room for Brooke when I was pregnant with her and somehow this bothered me more. Bob would help around the house with the children and the dishes and washing clothes and folding and putting them away. I just sat in the swing and swung and cried. I told Sarah, "Here I am almost thirty-nine and pregnant, my mom was a grandmother at this age."

Bob tried to console me, but I was having a difficult time with my anger toward God. The anger turned into pouting. I had always wanted another child but not now! I had not even prayed for another child. When I had told my parents about the pregnancy, they were very concerned about my age and the fact of having a C-Section in Italy. I was not enthused about having this child either, let alone in this country where I had heard nightmare stories about childbirth. Bob offered to send me home but I did not want to go to the states without my girls and him for four months. My due date would be around Christmas and I certainly did not want to leave my girls then.

My first appointment with Dr. Franco was in July. We had managed to purchase an old car when we moved to Gaeta. The shocks were terrible on the car so it was a very rough ride to Rome. We had taken the girls to summer camp, and then went to spend the night with Ross and Sarah the night before my appointment.

When we arrived at the doctor's we had to walk up four flights of steps to his office. The receptionist greeted us and asked us to wait in the waiting room. We had been there about ten minutes and I stood up and all of a sudden I started hemorrhaging. It scared me to death as I flew to the bathroom. I came out and told Bob what was going on, and he called the receptionist. She said, "Oh don't worry everything will be alright." I told her she did not understand that I was pregnant. With that she turned white as a ghost and called for the doctor. He came out and asked me a couple questions and said he would be with me shortly. I went back to the bathroom and fear filled my heart. The Lord spoke to me and said, "Do you want this child or not?" For the first time I saw that I had been acting like a spoiled brat and that God's way is not our ways, but His ways are perfect. "Yes, Lord, Yes! Whatever your will for me is, that is what I want! I am sorry for being so angry at you, please God, don't let me lose this child!" God had a way of getting my attention and I was really sorry for not trusting Him.

When I came out of the bathroom I had to wait about five minutes and the doctor called me and Bob into his examine room. He determined that I was losing some tissue, but he did not think I had lost the baby. He sent me over to have a sonogram to make sure that the baby was fine. We could see the heart beating and everything seemed to be okay. The problem was the same as I had with Amanda and Brooke, placenta privia. The placenta was on the bottom of the uterus. I was put on bed rest until the bleeding stopped which was about three days. The ride in the rough car probably aggravated it, but God got my attention real fast. He would help me through the next five months as He would be my strength.

I would like to say that I had learned so much about faith and trusting the Lord, that I lived the rest of my life in total victory, that my faith had taken me so far that I could soar high above the eagle and that I never questioned God again. That would be far from the truth, because God still had much for me to learn. I thought I had learned to trust God through this entire ordeal, but when the tests continued, I kept failing. There are a lot of things I can learn quickly, but it seemed that my ability to trust God completely and explicitly was yet to be learned. I still wanted ownership of myself and if things did not go according to the way I thought they should, I would question God. I have always had a problem questioning authority. Little did I know about myself and what He was trying to achieve in me.

CHAPTER XVIII

COULD I POSSIBLY KNOW MORE THAT GOD?

Isaiah 55:8 *For my thoughts are not your thoughts, neither are your ways my ways, saith the Lord.*

The apartment was too small for the five of us. There was not a single space to put a crib. The apartment could not have been more than eight hundred square feet. There was more room in the back yard than in the house. So the search began to find a more spacious living arrangement. Day after day we would go looking, and one day we found it. It was a gorgeous three story apartment in a gated community. The bottom floor had a huge room with an outside entrance, a private bathroom and bedroom. That would have been great for meetings and if we had guests. The next floor was the living room, dining room, and kitchen with a fireplace and a balcony. The upstairs had three large bedrooms and a bath. We filled out the papers for a contract, but the landlady would not accept it. She did not want us to rent the apartment because we were not military. She said she needed a guarantee of payment and since we were not military there was no guarantee we would pay. We showed her all our documents and told her that she would have nothing to worry about, but the answer was still "No!"

I could not understand. "God this would be a perfect place to have a church. You have made a mistake, why can't you work things out for us to get this place?" I prayed night and day, but the answer was still "NO."

Again, I could not understand God in all this. I did not like being told no when I thought I knew what was best. Why could God not see this would be perfect and change the mind of the landlady? Once again I thought I knew better than God. You may be thinking, "But you are a missionary." Well, God was teaching me to trust Him in all things and I was having a hard time with learning to trust Him. I had never before learned how to trust Him fully, and these were my testing grounds.

We did find another place just behind our apartment. It was high on a hill and over looked the bay. It was nice, and large, with lemon trees around the house. The balcony was huge about seventy foot long and thirty foot wide. We moved in right away and there were no problems renting our other apartment. But I was still angry that we did not get the nicer apartment. Three months later we heard that the apartment that I had wanted so badly had blown up killing the renter's dog. There was a shortage in the electricity and a gas leak. The family was not at home at the time since they were in the military. I would have been there with the children! *"Oh, God, Create in me a clean heart and renew a right spirit within me. Hear my cry, O God; attend unto my prayer. From the end of the earth will I cry unto thee, when my heart is overwhelmed; lead me to the rock that is higher than I. For thou hast been a shelter for me and a strong tower..."* Psalms 61:1-3

Boy was I wrong! God did know best after all, and He showed me that His ways are not my ways. How could I ever question Him again? He knew what was best for me and He had protected me and my children from sure death. How many times had He sheltered and protected us that we did not even know about? We are so unaware of his guardian angles.

The couple who took our apartment, Jim and Diana, became friends instantly. Diana was so kind and very respectful of our being missionaries. She helped me a lot with the girls and would give me gifts from the commissary in Naples. I had never met anyone so kind-hearted.

Bob had tried unsuccessfully to get Liberty University to keep up with the correspondence course he signed up for to finish his Masters, but the mail was just too slow and it would take months to even get a paper graded. We just could not understand why he could not get the college to respond. After many attempts to resolve the problems, Bob finally gave up on trying to do the correspondence courses.

Diana spent a lot of time at our house since her husband was on ship. Sometimes he would go out for days at a time. She was lonely and this gave us great opportunity to get close and talk. We talked a lot about her past and I was trying to understand why she was agnostic. She just could not believe in a personal relationship with God if there was a god. She was very candid and open, but I just could not penetrate her belief about God.

Time seemed to have passed so slowly while I was pregnant. I could not sleep and was miserable the last trimester. Dr. Franco set my delivery date for December 19. We had discussed about having the baby at the International Hospital where he could re-tie my tubes. At any other hospital he would have to get a court order since birth control was against the law. On the eighteenth we drove to Ross and Sarah's house to let the girls off and then Bob took me to the hospital. What would I do without them? They had become our family.

We were met in the lobby by a doorman. Soon nuns came and took us to a hospital room. Bob was nervous because this did not look like your everyday run of the mill hospital. He sat the bag down and said, "Don't touch anything, we may be leaving. Don't even sit on the bed." He went away to find someone to talk to about the room and when he came back, he said, "Okay, let's go!"

"What do you mean let's go" I cried. "I have got to have this baby. I can't stay pregnant." When we got out to the car Bob said they wanted about six thousand dollars for me to have the baby there, and I understood, because we did not have that kind of money.

Back to Ross and Sarah's we drove and were met with a surprise on their faces. I had not prepared to stay at their house, and it was cold. It was late so I went to bed to stay warm and cried myself to sleep. The next morning Bob and Ross took off to go find a hospital where I could have the baby that day. Several hospitals did not want to bother with me and one said they could not do it until Monday; they had a staff Christmas party planned that day. Before they arrived home, the doctor called and asked me what I had to eat, which was tea and some toast. He told me to meet him at the hospital at 2:00 p.m. He had already talked with Bob. I was scared, because I did not know what was in store for me in this country, and although I trusted Dr. Franco, I was not sure of his ability. Could he do as good a job with the C-section as I had in the states?

Although I had faith in God, at this point in my life my faith only went so far. I thought that certain things could be in our power, not in God's. I had not yet realized that God was in control of all things in my life and I did not know how to trust Him fully. Pleasing God was impossible for me, because I was void of faith in Him to know what was best for me. Hebrews 11:6 *"But without faith it is impossible to please God"*

I had been praying for an easy time with the delivery, but when I walked into the hospital I was deeply concerned for my recovery. When I sat on my bed for the mid-wife to prep me for surgery, I knew I was in trouble. The bed was an old iron bed with springs. When I sat on the bed it sank down three feet and I could not get back up without help. I thought to myself, how in the world will I ever get out of this bed with a C-Section? The mid-wife came back and got me ready and they wheeled me to surgery.

There were about twenty people around me; I was the subject of their studies that day I suppose. I kept asking if they were going to put a catheter in, I was concerned that they really did not know what they were doing. The mid-wife rammed it in my bladder seconds before I was out. Then something very strange occurred to me.

All of a sudden I could feel this intense pain like I had never felt before. I was going toward a light and I sense a voice say, "Jane, I can take all this pain away from you and give you peace." And the pain went away and I had never felt such peace in all my life. It was ecstasy. I said, "Lord, I can not go now, I have three girls to raise and I do not want them to be without a mother."

The awful pain came back and I heard the doctor calling my name. I was still in the operating room. I went in and out as I could hear the people in the room talking and laughing, and wondered if they were laughing at me. They wheeled me out and back down to my room where Bob was waiting. Dr. Franco told him I was fine and the baby girl was fine as I drifted in and out of consciousness and between moaning with agonizing pain. He said to Bob, "I don't understand why she is in so much pain." And he left.

Bob stayed with me until 11:00 p.m. and sat and held my hand, but he could do nothing. They would not give me anything for pain and when I asked they said it would keep me from healing. Once they came and gave me a shot, but it must have been water because the pain did not stop. I was so thirsty and sipped on water to keep me cool, but they found out that Bob had given me water and took that away from me and said that water would cause me more pain. I laid there all night praying, that was all I could do. The next day the temperature was down to zero outside and Bob had not gotten to the hospital yet. In fact, I had not seen my baby either. I was hurting so bad I did not care if I saw her or not, but they said if I wanted to see her, she would need clothes.

I called Bob and told him to go by the store and pick some clothes up for Kelly before he came to the hospital. About two hours later he brought some clothes in and the nurse clothed her and brought her to me. She said she had already had a bottle, so I asked her not to give her another bottle; I was going to nurse her. When she brought her again, she would not nurse, and I asked if she had eaten and the nurse said she had. Again, I asked her not to give her a bottle. Through the night they brought her several times and they had already fed her. The next morning when they brought her I told them not to feed her and the mid-wife argued with me, saying that I did not have milk yet. I explained to her that I had colostrum first then the milk would come and that was the way God designed it. They were angry at me but they did not give Kelly another bottle and I was the only woman on the floor who could nurse her child. They had told everyone else they could not nurse because they did not have milk. The gross ignorance of these people astounded me.

On the third day, I asked Bob if he would go down to our house in Gaeta and get me some Tylenol, I could not stand the pain any longer. I had not slept for the pain was unbearable. After I took the Tylenol I began to feel some relief. That night I woke up and I had messed all over myself. What had they given me? I could not believe I had done that in my sleep. I called and the mid-wife came in and I had to explain to her that I did not know what was happening. I still could not get out of the bed. No one came to help me get up or make me get up. My back hurt and I had pulled my shoulder from trying to move around on that cot. I could not get out of that hole in the bed. The next time I called for the mid-wife she brought me the bed pan. I have never been so embarrassed and humiliated in all my life. I just cried as she cursed and said awful things. I cried because I could not express in Italian how I felt at that moment and how I felt they were treating me. I just kept silent. The next time I had to go I knew it and I prayed and asked God to give me the strength to get out of that bed. I kept repeating, "I can do all things through Christ who strengthens me." I called for a nurse and she came and steadied me as I got up and I thought I would pass out. This was the first time I had stood on my feet since I went into surgery four days earlier. I could hardly walk to the bathroom next door, but I made it with the Lord's help.

The next few days as I lay in the bed, reading my Bible and praying and often crying, I asked the Lord why was I there? What purpose did I have being there because I could not even witness effectively for Him? I did not know the language well enough to strike up a conversation about God's grace and forgiveness of sin. "God can you show me your purpose in all this?" I prayed.

Each day I gained a small amount of strength and Dr. Franco was coming to evaluate my progress to see if I could go home. I would go out and try to walk the hall so I could make it to the elevator when he would release me from the hospital. Sometimes I could only make it to the bathroom and back. The woman in the bed beside me said very little to me. She had something wrong and would stay in the hospital for 1 month until the Baby was born. One morning when the nurses were cleaning up her side of the room and changing her sheets, I heard them talking about me. They said, "Well, at least her (talking about me) religion means something to her. She never complains or curses." God showed me that I was a witness for him although I could not effectively speak out for Him. I was humbled by the thought that my actions spoke louder than words.

Finally on Friday I could make it to the elevator and the doctor would be coming any time. When he came he took out my stitches. They had not used cat gut stitches in the States for years, it was plain to see how far behind this country was. He also had to remove a drainage tube. I thought I would pass out at that. We talked and I pointed out two knots in my veins in my right leg that had not been present when I arrived. I knew it was blood clots, because I had lain in the bed too long without movement and because they had not prepped me before surgery with surgical hose. Since the doctor trained in the states he should have known to have done that. He did not want me to go home, but at last he said he wanted to see me in a week and gave me a prescription for some cream to put on the clots.

Home never looked so good to me, although I could not do much. The girls were so excited because now we could have Christmas. Jim and Diana came up and brought lunch and we had a wonderful time. Diana was so considerate and tried to help in any way she could. She even gave me a shower with the few people that we knew.

Amanda and Brooke became little mommies and helped me so much with Kelly. They changed her diapers and brought her to me when she was hungry. Kelly looked so tiny in that basinet and even smaller in the beautiful baby bed Diana let me borrow. She had bought me new crib bumpers, matching comforter and sheets. It seemed that Diana could not do enough for us, for which I was extremely grateful.

I went back to Dr. Franco a week later and I had not gotten the prescription filled for the blood clot. He told me he wanted to see me again in a couple weeks and the blood clots better be going away or he would put me back in the hospital. As soon as I got home we had the prescription filled and I started using it. I was surprised that the medication did work, and the clot started to dissolve. Recovery took some time since I had a rough time in the hospital.

CHAPTER XIX

A TEST OF BROTHERLY LOVE

⌣∶∼

Acts 28:27 For the heart of this people has grown dull.

Don and Melinda were some missionaries we had met at Ross and Sarah's house one time when we were visiting them. They wanted to come down from Florence and work with us in Gaeta. The Italians in Gaeta were not open to the gospel and the people were not nearly as friendly as in Naples. However, we thought we might be able to join our efforts together and start a work in this area. We talked often and prayed and they prayed about coming down to our area. In January 1987, a month after Kelly was born they decided to join with us in the ministry there. When they came they stayed with us for 3 months until they could find a place of their own. That was quite a strain on our home life and family.

After they moved to a place of their own we felt that this idea really was not a good match and probably would not work out after all. We did not share the same thoughts, ideas, philosophy, Biblical views, or much of anything else. Don did not want to pass out the Bibles we had purchased because they were not King James Version. But the King James Version was English and they only had the Dio Dati translation which was in Italian. We could not see eye to eye on much of anything. We did remain friends although it was very uncomfortable at times. Their children were not allowed to even be normal children. They lived in the strictest environment along with their mother. Many years later we found out that he was abusive and the family was a shamble and a disgrace within the confines of their home.

For almost a year we had tried to work with Don, but he was very uncooperative. He thought everything we did was wrong. His approach as he visited folks in their homes was so aggressive they asked for him not to return. This was not the approach we had with the nationals. We genuinely loved the folks and tried to help anyway we could. As opportunity arose we shared the gospel with them and invited them to study the Bible. We tried to apologize for Don and his way of handling people and tried to talk with him, but he was stubborn and only his way was right.

It seemed that we were getting no where with the people in Gaeta or anywhere with Don. There was not the open hearts we had prayed so desperately for God to open. This was a beautiful area, but "their ears were hard of hearing, and their eyes they had closed, lest they should understand with their heart and turn,"(Acts 28:27) We had passed out tracts, visited people in their homes, started a Bible study with the children and numerous things, but no one was interested.

Bob and Ross had gone down to a little town to preach in an American work in San Vito. It is located in the heel of the boot. The American Church wanted to meet some of the missionaries on the field and talk to them about the work they were doing. Then they went back another time and God prompted Bob to go there to start a work with the Italians in that area. We thought that it might be good for our relationship with Don and Melinda if we moved anyway.

We had planned a quick trip home for Christmas to settle some business on the mobile home and visit family. We wanted everyone to see Kelly and to see how much Mandy and Brooke had grown. Cheri, Ross and Sarah's daughter, went with us on the trip back home. We drove to London so we could save money on the flight, but Kelly was sick all the way. We stayed a night in France and continued on our journey hoping to see a lot of sights on the way. But our time was limited and all we could see was a few majestic snow covered mountains in Switzerland. Bob almost got us killed on the streets of London driving on the wrong side of the road.

Flying was not my forte and as usual I was reluctant about the flight. When the plane took off my heart flipped over and I prayed for safety (and for my nerves) but I was not the only one. There was a lady who was sitting in front of us and as the plane took off, she slid out of her seat into the floor and had her rosary in her hand, just praying as hard as she could move those beads. I was trusting that God would be the wind under the wings and that He would keep the airplane in the air. Kelly continued to throw up on the plane.

Once we were at home we found out that the people that had purchased our mobile home had not paid the house payment in four months. Our bank account was drained. My dad had just evicted them before we came home, so we were left with making the decision to let the mobile home go back to the dealer. We knew it would be on our credit rating for the next seven years but we had no choice. The owners of the Mobile Home Park would not allow anyone to rent homes in their park.

It was such a joy to see our families. Everyone adored Kelly to death. We stayed with my parents although the house was so small. My mom was so concerned that Kelly was still throwing up so often, but we could not figure out why. She wanted me to take her to the doctor, but I really didn't see the need since she was okay otherwise.

All the way back to London, Kelly threw up several times on me. I smelled revolting when we landed. We were very exhausted when we disembarked. Bob got our car out of storage and we headed toward France. We just wanted to get across the English Channel before dark. We drove up to the dock ready to get on and our tire went flat. We had to turn around and get it fixed. Once on the ferry we all passed out for the one hour trip across the channel. It was late when we arrived in France and found a place to stay for the night. The cheap motel we liked had no front desk. You pass your credit card though a slot and the door opens and you have been assigned to a room. It was really quite unique.

We had two rooms, one for us and Kelly and one for Mandy and Brooke. The girls had been feasting on M&M's their grandmothers had given them so they were wired. They had been playing around and been silly for hours before they knocked on my door. They had locked themselves out of their room when they went to the bathroom. Bob and Kelly were asleep and I did not want to wake them so I stepped out in the hall with them. I could not figure out what to do at 2:00 a.m. I could not speak French so we stood in the little entrance way of the hotel not knowing what to do. I was in my housecoat, racking my brain trying to come up with an idea. I had just about concluded that we would have to sit up all night until Bob got up, when a man entered the hotel. He looked a little surprised when I approached him and asked if he spoke English. He didn't, so I tried Italian. He didn't speak Italian either. So I used my imagination and acted out a little play. He understood and called a clerk that was on duty upstairs and could automatically unlock the door from their quarters. I was so relieved that we could get back into the room, and get to sleep.

When we arrived in Gaeta we immediately prepared to move to San Vito. Ted Woodruff drove up from San Vito with his van and we packed it and rented another one and filled it up. It took three trips down to San Vito to move everything.

This area of Italy was absolutely the most unattractive place I had ever seen. It was not what I had pictured in my mind as to what Bob described. Nothing could have prepared me for how disappointed I felt when we arrived in San Vito.

CHAPTER XX

THE OPENED DOOR

ᴗ:ᴗ

II *Corinthians 2:12b "...A door was opened to me by the Lord."*

Our seventeenth move took us to a small house on Via Van Gogh and it was right on the street. Kelly was now fourteen months old and I was concerned that she could and would run out the front door and into the street, which she did several times. Being right on the street we could not open our windows for all the traffic and dust. Bob had rented the house on one of his trips down there and like any man didn't really check everything out. He had tried to describe the area and house, but when I first saw it I was not pleased. We had no water pressure and could not take a bath. We were attached to a garage that worked on diesel trucks ten hours a day. Starting early in the mornings you could hear the engines and smell the diesel fumes. San Vito was probably the most depressing place I had ever been and the topography was about the ugliest I had ever seen. None of the other towns close by were appealing either. The girls often joked that the town, San Vito di Normani, (the official name of the town) should really be named San Vito di Nienti (San Vito of nothing).

Since the house was unbearable we lived there only a few months. We found a little house in the country side. After we moved in the landlord became very difficult to deal with. He rode our backs constantly over every little thing. He got mad because I let the children play in the water when it was over one hundred degrees outside. He would not move his guard dog from the back of the house until Bob got bit. He wanted the driveway swept clean everyday. He was a terrible old man and a law breaker as well. He had been sited several times for selling vegetables that he had fertilized with human waste from his sewer.

As soon as we got to San Vito we began attending the American Church. This gave me an outlet since I had no Christian fellowship with other believers when we lived in Gaeta. It was good to have conversation with ladies that I could understand and grow close to. Amanda and Brooke also made close friends once again with the Woodruff's daughters and they would often spend the night with each other. It also was great fellowship for us as well having someone to talk to about what God was doing in our lives.

In the American Church we met a young gentleman who had made a terrible mistake. He came to us and poured out his heart. He was up for promotion in the military and they had to do a clearance check on him and he had to fill out a report with many personal questions. One of the questions was, "Have you ever taken drugs?" He wanted to do the honest thing since he had now accepted the Lord as his Savior. So he answered, "Yes". When he went on leave back to the U.S. a year previously, he had smoked marijuana at a party. When the paper work went through for the approval, not only did he not get the promotion but he was discharged from the military. He was very heart broken, needless to say, but he had been trying to tell the Italian family that he had been very close to what had happened and they could not understand what he was saying. He wanted to tell them why he was leaving, but more importantly why he told the truth to the military and what a difference Christ had made in his life. He wanted Bob to interpret the message of salvation to this family.

Bob went with Tony to see the Giuliani family and had a great time talking with them and their four boys. They listened intently and invited Bob and me to come back to talk with them again over dinner. We went and not only were they there but they had invited other families. There were about twenty of us in all and after we finished eating, they asked Bob to get up and tell everybody what he had told them earlier about salvation. So Bob stood up and began to preach to them about what they needed to hear concerning the gospel. They wanted to hear more and so another family wanted us to come to their house to invite others in and have a bible study. Several nights a week we would have a bible study and each night was in a different town. Each town was in close proximity to each other only about 15 miles apart. The people were so friendly and wanted to hear more every time we met with them.

It was very clear that God had a job for us to do in San Vito. We were so amazed to see the excitement and hunger for the Word of God in the people in this area. This was an open door to many homes and opportunities to reveal the grace of God unlike we had witnessed before. Within a few months we were able to rent a building and had a regular meeting place. On the sign outside the building we wrote in Italian, John 8:32 *"YOU SHALL KNOW THE TRUTH AND THE TRUTH SHALL SET YOU FREE."*

One little lady in her seventies began attending our worship services. Alda was a wonderful Christian woman who came to know our Lord when she was about sixty-four years old living in Africa. Alda grew up in Italy as a young child and moved to Scotland with her parents in her teens so her father could find work. She married an Englishman while she was in Scotland. He was in the military and was transferred to Africa. He died while in Africa and left her with two small children. She was teaching English to some Italians who had come to Africa to work. She began to learn Italian from them and met a man from Italy and fell in love with him and they married. He acquired some land and they had a big plantation and she often told me of their workers.

Her sister-in-law and brother-in-law also lived there. One day her sister-in-law invited her to come to a bible study and Alda went. She had seen the changes in the life of her in-laws and nephew. They began to tell her of the freedom they had in Jesus Christ, so she invited her nephew to come speak to the workers on their plantation. As she began to listen, her heart was opened and she trusted Christ as her savior. Some time later they sold the land and moved back to southern Italy and she was so hungry for Christian fellowship she began to pray that God would send a missionary to San Vito to work among the people. She used to tell me these things as we would sit in her kitchen and have tea-time every week. She was the dearest Christian I had ever known outside Mrs. Delnay.

She called me "Jana" and loved for me to come visit her. Often she would remind me that Bob and I were her answer to prayer. She seldom got away from home because it was very difficult for her to walk because of crippling arthritis. Every time we had services we would pick her up and she would love to come and sing praise to God. Our moral support came from Alda and she was our greatest prayer warrior. Alda grieved often that Rocco, her husband, would not listen to her pleas to trust in God alone and to receive Christ as Savior. He was even more determined to be as Catholic as he could be. The last time I saw Alda, she said she would be praying for us and she put an Ivory necklace around my neck and said she did not have much, but she wanted me to have her necklace from Africa. I have the fondest memories of that dear sweet woman, which has now moved her citizenship from this sinful world to Glory with our Heavenly Father. I am looking forward to seeing her again soon.

November of 1987 my mother, Bob's mother and his brother came over to visit us. We all were so excited as we drove to Rome. The drive was about ten hours, but well worth the drive to pick our family up to visit. It was always fascinating to see the excitement on the faces of those who were out of the United States for the first time and this was Bob's mother's first time ever getting on a plane. I laughed so much when Bob's brother, Gary, told of their trip over on the flight. The stewardesses were going around asking if any one wanted to rent the ear devices for two dollars, in which my mom said "No, I don't think so" and Bob's mom added, "We brought chewing gum." They thought that they were for your ear's popping when the altitude changed. I could just imagine what that stewardess thought.

We took them down the Amalfi Coast, Pompeii, and the town of Trulli, all of which were in the south. There is just so much to see in Italy we could not possibly show them every thing in the two weeks that they were there. We had Italian friends to come in and they really loved our family. They fixed food and brought it to the house and were so hospitable. We all gathered in the kitchen where we had a fire to stay warm. My dad stayed home and ended up back in the hospital with his heart again. It was not bad, they just adjusted his medication.

When we took them back to Rome, we stayed at the Stumps' house since they were in the states at the time and were able to show them around as well. There was so much to see in Rome. There were the stairs that were suppose to have been those which Jesus walked up when he was brought to Pilot for trial. It was told in Catholicism that angels brought the stairs to Rome from Jerusalem and were told by the angels to build a church around them. The Catholics climb up these stairs on their knees even today, saying the rosary, to get forgiveness of sin. There was the Church of the Bones where the Capuchin Monks are buried in the basement of the church and when they have decayed they dig the bones up and clean them then decorate the church with the bones. Then there is the Vatican, with all its fanfare, splendor, massive marble floors, huge marble columns, beautiful marble statues, jeweled crowns, gold and ruby cups, and so much more. They were overwhelmed with all there was to see.

Tears were shed once again as we said goodbye at the airport. We knew Gary, Bob's brother, would take good care of our moms and they would be safe. We drove the long way back to San Vito and settled into our regular routine of visiting and having services for the Italians.

After about six months of living at the house on the outskirts of San Vito, we decided it would be best if we moved, so we found an apartment in the next town of Mesagna. Our landlord was so furious with us for moving. He wanted us to give him a thousand dollars to paint the house. It was because of him we were moving to begin with. He was constantly on our backs over everything. He even got all over us for using what he thought was too much water. But we were the ones that purchased the water. We bought and paid for it ourselves.

Bob told him "no" he would not give him the money, that we would paint it ourselves. We knew the paint could not be more than one hundred dollars. He became very enraged and almost hit Bob. He wanted the money, but Bob reminded him when we moved in that he said, if we wanted the house painted we could paint it and when we left, he would paint it. He made several threats but we were getting used to the anger we had seen played out in the lives of the Italians. They were very dramatic, but usually did nothing. It was interesting that God used poetic justice, and two months later he was electrocuted one night while pumping sewage on his garden.

CHAPTER XXI

THE INTRUDER

ᴗ:ᴗ

John 10:10 *The thief cometh not but to steal, and to kill, and to destroy; I am come that they might have life,*

Our next move was to the fourth floor of a small apartment building. It was a lovely apartment with lots of room. The building had only six apartments, and the parking garage was nice as well. It was a sheltered parking area in the back of the apartments. The girls each had their own desk that Bob had built for them to do their school work. Mandy had a room to herself and Brooke shared a room with Kelly.

We had a large living room with a dining area and beautiful tile floors. The only thing that frightened me were the balconies. With Kelly being so young, only two years old, I could just imagine her climbing over the railing, falling four stories. There was an elevator but we were used to walking up stairs, so we seldom used it. I really enjoyed the apartment; it was the nicest place we had lived in Italy. We could stand on the balcony and see for miles. We especially loved the view of the orchards when the trees began to bloom that spring.

One evening we had a lot of people in the apartment for a pizza party and there were several other children as well. I was sitting at the table and I felt the need to go check on Kelly. When I could not find her and saw that the window to her room was opened, I panicked. I just knew she had crawled up in the window and fell out. I called for Bob, but he could not find her either. We were in a fright, but we finally found her all by herself in the bathroom playing in the bidet with water pouring all over the floor, laughing and giggling. I picked her up and hugged her very tight and cried. I was so relieved that she was okay.

Kelly was like having my own grandchild. Often people would ask me if she was our grandchild which insulted me but I was proud to be a parent of a child so young. I was enjoying her more than I did Mandy and Brooke because now I was older and wiser and even had a lot more patience. She was probably spoiled by all of us but she was entertaining and a delight. How could I have been so angry with God when he wanted to bless my life so much? But don't we do that often, because we can not see the outcome of what we are going through. One day we were on the balcony and I was holding Kelly thinking how God had blessed me so much with the girls. Kelly put her little hands on my cheeks and looked at me square in the face and said, "Mommy, u beautiful!" Tears streamed down my face as I held her so close to my heart and thanked God for the blessing of having another child.

Our little church building was on the outskirts of town. We had about ten to fifteen adults coming to the services. For the most part we only had one couple that we knew was saved. The others were coming and were listening. They had many questions for us and the Lord was working in hearts. Among the group there was an extraordinary poor family that had us for dinner on several occasions and invited friends in to hear the gospel. They could not do enough for us as they were so appreciative for anything. Everyone that was coming to the church services was so curious about the Word of God. They wanted to know if it was true. Not many people in Italy had seen a Bible before. Once in Naples a man about seventy-five years old had asked Bob what book did he have in his hand, and Bob told him it was the Bible. The man asked to hold it because he had never seen a Bible. Bob gave him a Bible of his own so he could read it for himself. We would run into people we had given a tract to years earlier and they would pull it out and say, you gave this to me and I still have it and read it everyday. Italians for the most part in the south wanted to know what the Bible said, and we had no trouble telling them. We would often tell them, "We are human and we can make a mistake. You need to read the Word of God for yourselves and see what God says."

One New Years Eve we spent hours talking to Tony and Josephine a couple that had been coming for some time to the bible studies. They had been coming to our services and were wrestling with trying to understand what a true Christian was and how one could become one. We tried many times to help them understand that it took nothing but the Blood of Jesus Christ and they did not have to do anything except trust in Him. They just could not get to the point where they could accept that. They knew we were honest and that it was a characteristic of a true believer to be honest, and began to question how being a Christian would affect their business. Honesty is not revered as something anyone would desire in Italy. Everybody tried to scam someone else; it's the way of life. In Italy you trust no one.

After we had talked on several occasions, Tony and Josephine came to the conclusion that they could not see how they could make a profit or even live if they were honest with everyone and the government. I hope they received Christ later, because Josephine died about three years after that. She choked to death on the goiter that had been growing in her throat for years.

A woman down one floor from us had moved out of her apartment. We knew her somewhat because she was the pharmacist and often we would ask her questions instead of going to the doctor. I had learned much about how to take care of the children because at that time in Italy, you could ask for a medication and they would sell it to you over the counter. If you could name it you could purchase it.

She approached Bob one day and told him that our landlord had sold the apartment we lived in and would be asking us to move shortly, but she would rent her apartment to us. I questioned it and really did not want to move, but Bob just knew that she was telling the truth, so we moved again; this was our twentieth move. We did not have to load a van or rent a truck this time, but we did have to move everything one floor down to that apartment.

It was getting hot outside and inside. For the most part we were used to the heat and it was somewhat tolerable. But like any American we liked our fresh air. We went to bed on that May night and left the outside shade slightly open at the bottom so the cat could go outside on the balcony. He had been bothering us at night so I shut him up in the living room. At 3:45 a.m. I was awakened by a little tapping noise. I lay there with my eyes shut, thinking "How did that cat get out?" But it got closer and closer. I opened my eyes and saw, what I thought was Mandy, our oldest daughter, crawling on the floor. I said, "Mandy what are you doing in here?" The image of someone with a white tee shirt stopped and made no movement. Again I asked, "Mandy, you better answer me, what are you doing in here in the middle of the night?"

The image of a slender young person all stooped over in a cowardly position ran out of my bedroom. I sensed Bob was awake also and said, "Bob go get Mandy and see what she is up to!!" knowing that it did not look at all like her silhouette, but I could not comprehend who else could be in the house except the girls. Bob ran down the hall in the direction that the intruder ran. We heard the screen door to the balcony off the kitchen slam shut. I opened Mandy's bedroom door and turned the light on so I could see if she was in bed. I was so confused being awakened out of a dead sleep, I went over to her and shook her and asked, "Were you just in our room?" She said she was not, but I could not grasp the moment and demanded for her to tell the truth. Bob started calling for me and said someone had been in our garbage on the balcony, but when I reached him trying to go through the rubble, I could plainly see it was not garbage but the contents of our handbags.

Mandy was wide awake by now so we began to assess the situation. We clearly knew that there was no need to call the police from past experiences; they do not even bother to come! We had been robbed of only our money this time, about four hundred dollars. The whole situation was upsetting to say the least, but we were even more alarmed to know that he had been in the apartment for some time. He had eaten, and thrown peach seeds on the floor and put the cat on the back porch. He had to pass through Kelly and Brooke's room to put the cat out back. After dawn, Bob went down to the police station to report the theft. They knew that it was the caravan of gypsies on the out skirts of town, but they were not going to do anything about it. Quite a few people were robbed those several months that the gypsies lived there, and then it stopped when they traveled on. The police never interfered until one day someone saw one of them driving around town with his dead wife in the floor of the car, and then they went out and arrested him.

That night we realized the toll that the robbery took on us and how it changed our lives. We felt that our privacy had been truly intruded upon. Our sense of safety had been disrupted. We felt violated. Mandy could not sleep without a chair propped against her door. We awoke very often and got up to check all the doors and windows again and again. We realize that he could have killed us in our sleep, and that was scary. However, we knew God was in control and that nothing would harm us unless He allowed it. We were in His hands and we knew He cared for our safety and well being.

Throughout the summer months we worked closely with the youth that were in the community. Bob held Bible studies and worked with the kids to put on plays for the adults. The kids seemed to be having a lot of fun with Bob. A few other people joined in on attending the services.

Time was growing near for our furlough, a time when we could share with the churches what God was doing in Italy among the people. We had been in Italy almost four years this time. It was so exciting to see God at work among the Italians in this area. We genuinely cared and loved these folks, and they cared and loved us as well. The language was so difficult for me. Bob felt it also; he just could not ever express himself like he wanted to in another language. He studied and prayed in Italian but felt that he lacked the ability he needed. Maybe that was normal, but we would never be as good as Ross and Sarah in the language and that was frustrating to say the least.

We had called another missionary in the Naples area to see if he would want to oversee the ministry while we went home. He was delighted and moved down to the area of San Vito near Brendesi in August. We were not planning to go home until January or February of 1990. That would give us an opportunity to get Bart ready to take the ministry over. After Bart and his family moved, the time schedule changed somewhat for us to go home sooner. My niece was planning to get married in January and wanted us to be home for that. As God would have it, our time table was rearranged several times and we moved our leave time for December.

As we began to pray about the plans of returning, God directed our hearts back to northern Italy. We spoke to the missionary that came down to take our place and he was more than willing to continue with the church if we did not come back to that area. However, we thought our plans were shattered when one day Bart was out in his yard and got struck by lightening. It was a horrible experience and he had some nerve damage, but recovered considerably. Planning to return to northern Italy, God directed us to sell all of our household things once again. It was always so hard to sell everything we had and pick up and start all over again, but we had already done it so many times, it became natural. Besides we found that moving was more expensive than starting over.

Kelly was so young and she just could not understand people walking out of our house with her toys. I could not explain to her in a way she could understand why everything was gone. She seemed so broken hearted. How do you explain things like this to a child? You don't have the wisdom to make them understand, you trust God will convey His comfort to them. It is the same way when we have times when we do not understand what is going on. Proverbs 3:5-6 says we must look to Jesus and He will guide our ways when we do not understand. We need only to trust Him. He knows when our heart is broken and saddened. He sees each tear that falls.

We had to change our plans once again on the flight to October 5th. It seemed that God was moving fast in our plans to return home. We tried every way we could to sell the car but could not sell it because of a small technicality; they had misspelled our name on the title. We had to leave it behind with an Italian man who probably made money off it. I could not understand why we just could not sell it. We ended up losing money on the car and I questioned God again, and again. As much as we needed the money why could we not sell the car? Well, no answer ever came. Although it took me many years, I realized that some things are just not for us to know. But this I do know, *"For we do know that in all things God works for the good of those who love Him."* Romans 8:28

This was just another example of me wanting to have things in my control. I had a difficult time trusting God to control all things in my life. I wanted to control everything and could not easily understand that I was trying to control God and that I was trying to manipulate Him into doing what I thought needed to be done. Have you ever done that? Actually I thought I knew more than God. I did not admit that because I was in denial that this was a problem for me.

Toward the end of September our apartment was getting empty. Everything we had had been sold so quickly. We packed boxes and boxes of books, my china, and my towels to ship home. There was so much to do in preparation to leave and getting everything organized was orchestrated by God Himself. By nature I am not a well organized person. Moving everybody lock, stock and barrel was quite an ordeal, and as I look back I could not have done it without His help.

Soon the place was empty and we moved our things to Ted's house. He was going to take us to Rome to catch our flight the following day. It amazed me that everything seemed to be planned on a timetable, but I knew that we had only the puzzle pieces and it was God who was putting things together for us. It always seemed that way. We would be confused and uncertain and then somehow it would all come together and we would be so amazed. Only God could take the credit for the way every detail fell into place.

CHAPTER XXII

THE PITY PARTY

ᗌ:ᗏ

Peter 1:7 *That the trial of your faith, being much more precious than of gold that perisheth, though it be tried with fire, might be found unto praise and honor and glory at the appearing of Jesus Christ.*

With ten suitcases in hand and a cat in a carrier we headed to Rome where we would take our flight to Philadelphia, then on to Charlotte, North Carolina. This was a very difficult time for me all around. I had been fighting panic attacks since January and the break-in did not help matters either. It was a beautiful October morning and the weather was so pretty but when the plane took off I started crying. The frightful moment of lift-off overwhelmed me. One lady leaned over and said, "Don't worry honey, you will return one day to beautiful Rome, don't cry." I told her I was not crying because of leaving Rome, I was crying because I was scared to death of flying. There was just something about being all the way up in the sky, I did not like, and this time it really frightened me. We had some interesting landings as well that made me uncomfortable. One time the pilot almost overshot the runway. Another time the pilot had to do a trick turn to land.

Well, I was so glad when we finally touched down although the flight was smooth. When we landed in Charlotte it was very rough. We picked the cat up and his eyes were as big as saucers.

Mother and daddy had brought their motor home to pick us up. We needed it with all the luggage, cat and three girls. We were so excited to see everyone after almost four years but could hardly wait to hit the bed that night.

It seemed that we had a million and one things to do. First, we had to purchase a car to get around in and realized that a van would probably serve us well. We had been down to see Bob's family the Sunday we landed and told his mother we would bring the girls back in a few days to spend the night. We were still unwinding and resting from the trip but knew we would have to find a place to live soon, so we started looking at our options. We could live in Randleman, Bob's mother had some land beside her house we could use, but we really did not want to be way out in the middle of nowhere.

On Thursday the twelfth of October we took Amanda and Brooke to spend a few days with Bob's mother, Ruth. Kelly was so young almost three now, but with her still potty training, I felt it best if she did not go. She stayed with my mother while we took them the fifty mile trip. We ate lunch and stayed a little while so it was dark when we returned. I had a key to my parents' house so I let myself in and found a note on the kitchen bar which read, "Jane, there has been a terrible accident and Billy has been taken to the Baptist Hospital. Come over as soon as you get home; it is really bad."

Billy was my sister's son and lived only one eighth of a mile from my parents. He was sixteen and had only had his driver's license for six months. On the way I prayed that God would not take him. Billy was such a sweet kid. When we arrived at the hospital we told the attendant who we were and they ushered us to the family waiting room. My sister looked at me as I walked through the door and burst out crying; I knew he was gone. We hugged and I cried with her. I knew her pain was devastating. I had no words of comfort. I looked around with tears in my eyes and saw Kelly and she was reaching out for me. She was so frightened. It was more than a little child could comprehend. The days ahead were filled with the greatest sadness our family had ever known and there were many unanswered questions. And again, I could find no words to console my sister. What do you say? "Billy was a Christian and we knew that he was with the Lord." That was the greatest comfort any of us could have at a time like this, it was so very painful for all of us.

Kim, Becky's daughter, was in shock. She was so close to her brother, Billy. They did everything together. I was not sure if Kim was going to have a nervous breakdown or not. But through the Grace that God so liberally gave, we all managed the visitation and funeral as well as could be expected. Billy thought that no one liked him, but the line at the funeral home was a two hour wait to see the family. I think there was little sleep for any of us those horrifying days. My dad was so full of pain, and hurt. His only grandson, now gone. He literally cried for weeks and we thought his heart could not hold up under the stress. We knew dad's heart was wrenched with the pain of Billy's death.

The next few weeks were a mere blur as we all tried to pull our lives together. We knew that Becky, my sister and Bill, her husband, were having a horrendous time with the grief that they were experiencing and it would take many years before they could be normal again if that was possible. There would be nothing that would take that pain away except much time. No one can begin to imagine the pain associated with losing a child except God, who offered His son as a sacrifice for our sins, on Calvary. He knew what it was like to lose a child too. But His son did not stay dead, He arose again so that we could have the hope, the promise, that since He lives we can live also with Him in eternity. One day we will all see Billy again, and rejoice that we can share eternity together, because of what Christ has provided for us.

Bob and I had much to think about. Our large supporter, the man who owned the company in Ohio, was late on the support. Our bookkeeper called and asked if he should call them. Bob thought that would be a good idea but all that was said was that there was a problem with cash flow that month. They had been so good to us and had even increased our support when Kelly was born. They had never been late on support before.

One thing we had to consider was what we should do about housing. We prayed and asked the Lord to show us what to do. We looked into renting and purchasing. We thought that it might be a good investment to purchase a house instead of renting and throwing the money away. We could always rent a house to someone when we went back to Italy. It would also be nice to have a home when we retired. We began the search and found a modest home in a little community about seventeen miles south of Winston-Salem, in a little community called Welcome. It was amazing to see how God orchestrated all the right things at the right timing so we could purchase the house. We found some old furniture here and there and in yard sales and moved in the house the first part of December which was our twenty-second move if we count living with my parents for a short while. Every one of us were so excited to have a home of our own, and it even had a swimming pool, which I felt very guilty about. I could not believe that we actually owned the trees in the yard. It was truly a blessing from God.

The grocery store was amazingly close to the house and I had gone to get some light bulbs. While I was there I had a strange, very strange feeling that I was going to drop dead. I felt as if my heart had stopped beating and all of my strength had drained out of my body. I had to sit down on some boxes and a clerk came over and gave me some water. I checked out and drove home and told Bob what had happened then all of a sudden it hit me again. It scared me and I thought I was dying. There was no pain, but I was sure I was dying. I made Bob drive me to the hospital where the doctor on duty could see me having the attacks while I was on a monitor. Severe panic attacks were the diagnosis. He gave me a prescription and said I could go home. But I couldn't, and I told him I couldn't. I could not survive the night and asked if I could stay. They admitted me and gave me a sedative and I rested well. The next morning a psychiatrist came in and talked with me. He wanted me to tell him every thing I had encountered within the last year. I began to tell him about our robbery and the hormone changes, the packing and moving and how the flight affected me and my nephew getting killed. The stress of purchasing a house and moving so many times, and he said that it was no wonder I had panic attacks. I had nothing left in my body to handle stress. I was released with medication, but suffered extreme difficulty in leaving the house for anything for several months. I was afraid of having another attack. I remember the first time I left the house and the strange feeling that came over me. I had to find Bob quickly, and then I was okay. It took me a few more months before I was totally comfortable with being alone.

In January our support was a little late again. So Bob called to Ohio. He did not want to appear to be desperate, but wondered if there was something wrong. They said, they were having some problems and we needed to pray for them, but did not elaborate. We could not imagine what was going on, but knew that it did not sound good. In February we got a call and they said that they had to file bankruptcy and they could not send us anymore money. Our hearts sank to our stomachs. What on earth are we going to do? We just purchased a car and a house. Their support was almost seventy percent of our income. We prayed and knew we had to trust the Lord through all this, although it took a toll on our lives. We were not prepared for all God had in store for us to learn through trial after trial.

Bob had to find a job quickly, because we had bills coming in. Once again we had no savings to fall back on. It had taken all of our income to live on and to travel back home and a down payment on the house. Bob was thankful that the government was taking the Census that year, because that was the job God provided for him. He knew it was a short term job, only eight months. Once again, we contacted our supporting churches and told them we could not go back to Italy right now. We did not know what were going to do, but somehow we had to survive. Once again we told them to drop our support until we could determine what God wanted.

We felt no direction from God at all about returning to Italy at that time. We were so consumed with making ends meet we wondered if God was through with us. I saw the pain in Bob as he was so heartbroken not to be serving God in the way he wanted. He taught Sunday school for the singles at our church, but was disappointed that they seemed so passive about serving God and had no outreach. There was no real excitement in the ministry at that church. People would ask what we were planning to do and we really did not have a clue what the future held for us now. Deputation really did not work in our favor and seemed to exhaust all of our resources. Each trip home we lost our support and we were emotionally exhausted.

We put Mandy and Brooke in public school. North Davidson was supposed to be the best school around anywhere, but Mandy was very distraught. She complained that all the teachers did was try to get control of the class for most of the day. Once she could get control she assigned homework. They were used to home schooling and not used to the foolishness, lack of respect and the discipline problems that prevail in our public schools. They had real culture shock when they came home to the states and went to school. Mandy said she wanted to go back to home schooling, so we pulled her out and she did that for the rest of the school year. Brooke on the other hand was a social butterfly. She enjoyed the interaction with her peers. She was not careful with those she associated with and we began to notice changes in her behavior that we did not like.

I applied to the school system the next fall to be a substitute teacher and made some much needed money. One day I had to substitute for one of Brooke's teachers. It was a science class and the teacher said all I needed to do was give them a test. Brooke did not want the students to know I was her mother, because they would rib her over that so I did not tell anyone. When I went into the room the students were so disrespectful and saying all kind of dirty things. I could not believe this environment or what I was hearing. The test was on human reproduction and one of the discussion questions on the test was appalling. **"Please discuss in detail how the female becomes pregnant."** I could not believe my child of fifteen years olds had to discuss these issues with a male teacher in detail even though it was in writing. I was determined that day that the next fall I would take her out of public school. Mandy was already in a private high school called Salem Academy. It was her choice and she wanted to go there. It was not a Christian school but it was a college prep school. Mandy was challenged in tremendous ways there. She hated it at first because it was so very difficult and demanding, but the second year she adjusted to the five to six hours of homework every night.

The work at the Census Bureau had ended, so Bob started painting for a friend. God kept us well and healthy through all of those years without insurance. After about one and a half years of painting, a man at the church we attended offered him an opportunity to be a sales representative for his company and Bob took the job. He worked long and hard hours and worked at times when he was sick with a fever and could hardly stand up. He knew if he did not work, we had no money. I worked a few hours a week in the office, so we were able to pay our bills and had money to buy groceries, but it was a still a struggle and we still had no insurance.

We had been working there for some time and Bob was finally beginning to clear about four hundred dollars a week and sometimes made as much as five hundred dollars. His sales had begun to pay off in the second year of working there, but this made the boss angry, because sometimes Bob made as much as him. He began to make demands on Bob that were unreasonable. He asked him to make sales tapes for the other sales people, and there was no other time for him except after midnight. Bob told him that he worked enough hours and that on his off time he wanted to spend it with his family. This did not set well with his boss. One day Bob told him he was crazy for making demands that were unreasonable and he fired Bob. I could not continue working there for him, so I left as well.

On the way home, as I drove alone, I felt like I just had to scream. I just had to scream where no one but God could hear me. I could not hear God's gentle voice, "Trust Me" I was too caught up with the noise I was making and worrying about how we were going to make it. How much more could we, I, take. I knew that what we were experiencing was not hidden from the girls, and I knew they saw our pain once again as we struggled for understanding. What was this going to do to them? To us, to me? "Dear God! What is going to become of us now? Have you brought us into this desert to die?" Many sleepless nights, we lay in bed and prayed for answers, but answers came by the way of provisions and Bob had a job within a week with a restaurant equipment company. He was back down to three hundred dollars a week. We managed to survive although it was extremely difficult. Once again

I became angry with the way our lives were turning out. The tests were becoming unbearable and I was failing them rapidly. What was God trying to do to us? Although my trials were not as harsh as losing my children, I felt *"What strength do I have, that I should hope? And what is my end, that I should prolong my life? Is my strength the strength of stones: or is my flesh bronze? Is my help not within me? And is success driven from me?"* Job 6:11 -13

My heart and mind was not on the scripture, I was too busy bathing in self-pity, again. And the pity party was for the most part in private. I did not want anyone to know that I could not have victory over feeling sorry for myself and so I played the role of being contented with what ever the Lord handed me although I was miserable inside. This just does not work with the true Christian. You have to be contented in knowing that God does not make mistakes and that suffering plays an essential role in the life of faith. It is not the result of sin or bad choices on the part of a believer like I thought. I was all too consumed in wondering what others thought of our situation. I was so afraid that my parents and our families would think we were not successful and that we were poor examples of God's servants and a disgrace. I knew I needed an attitude adjustment, but I also thought I deserved to be angry at what life handed us. I compared myself to others who were so successful in the ministry and who were successful at material gain. I was on a merry-go-round and could not get off.

My greatest question was why? I did not see that these were trials that God had designed for my benefit. I called out to God and told Him every pain I was feeling. I hid nothing from Him. He knew my heart anyway and hiding was not possible. He knew my every thought and saw each tear. Yet He loved me still.

I was rebelling against the trials and had been all my life. I had not purposed in my heart to have the mind of Christ.

Thinking right was necessary to having the same attitude as Christ had. In II Corinthians 10:5b, it says to *"Bring every thought into captivity to the obedience of Christ."* Had not God *"chosen the poor of this world to be rich in faith and heirs of the kingdom which he promised to those who loved Him?"* James 2:5 Why should I expect more? Wasn't I rich? God had left me an example in I Peter 2:21 - 24 *"For to this you were called, because Christ also suffered for us, leaving us an example, that you should follow His steps.... who when He was reviled, did not revile in return; when He suffered, He did not threaten, but committed Himself to Him who judges righteously;"*

In I Peter 4:1 we see that *"since Christ suffered for us in the flesh, (we are to) arm ourselves also with the same mind."* In verse two it says that suffering actually enables us to live in the will of God, but I was yet to grasp this concept. I could not honestly say with Job, *"Though He slay me, yet will I trust Him"* Job 13:15. I was all too consumed about what others thought, especially my parents. I was forty-six years old and I still was craving my parents' approval. All I wanted from my family was understanding and respect and that was one thing they could not give us. There always seemed to be plenty of respect for others in the ministry, but somehow my parents could not see God at work in our lives; they only saw failure. They could never understand our suffering as God working in our lives and the focus being on what we were learning from all this, that God is sovereign over all. We did not realize it but God was enlarging our concept of Himself. We were learning to trust in His goodness and power even through the worst of times.

Sometimes we would lose all hope, me more than Bob. Time after time I felt defeated but God kept me from despair. Bob never gave up. He stayed faithful no matter what. Oh, there were times of disappointment and struggle, but he remained true to his faith and trust in His Lord. I had never seen the gentle, quite strength that Bob possessed in anyone else. He never complained about our situation, but took every step for what it was worth. He had set his hope fully on God's Grace and held on for whatever came next. I felt many times that God did not like us or "had it in for us." My personality was just that different from Bob's. It would take many more years and many more trials yet for me to release my resentment and to trust God completely.

CHAPTER XXIII

RUNNING AHEAD OF GOD

~:~

Isaiah 40:31 *But they that wait upon the Lord shall renew their strength; they shall mount up with wings like eagles; they shall run, and not be weary; and they shall walk, and not faint.*

One morning while driving down the highway to Winston-Salem Bob and I saw a big sign about a church. The sign said, THE CHURCH YOU HAVE BEEN LOOKING FOR. Well, we were looking for a church home so that sign was appealing. That Wednesday night we decided to visit. We went back on Sunday and every Sunday since that September in 1992.

We did find the church we had been looking for. Pinedale Christian Church fulfilled our inter most desire to worship our Lord and Savior. For the first time in our lives we felt that we **had** truly worshiped God. There was nothing extraordinary **about** the people. They were loving, kind and full of compassion. There was not anything astonishing about the ministerial staff. However, God was present in every meeting. The unity was amazing. We all joined in one accord to worship our God. It was amazing how God worked in our hearts through the communion time, the worship time and in the message of His word. Within one month we became part of their family.

My parents loved going to Florida in the winter months and January 1994 was no exception. They had made numerous friends from all over and their favorite place to go was Melbourne. They took their motor home and rented a spot in a resort area where they enjoyed getting out and being with their friends. They usually spent their anniversary in February soaking up the sun. One day my mother called and said that dad had a massive heart attack and was not expected to live. My sister and I asked if we should come down and she said no that dad probably would not make it anyway by the way the doctors were talking. She would bring his body back when he passed. However, dad did pull through and my sister went down to be with mother and to drive the motor home back. Becky stayed until my dad recovered and was well enough to make the trip back home.

Ross and Sarah had moved back to the States now and we often got together since we both were from Winston-Salem, North Carolina. This evening they had invited us over to cook out and I was to bring potato chips. We were running a tad late so I asked Bob to drop me off and I would run into the grocery store while he went about six blocks away to pick up Amanda and Brooke at the church. They had been to a teen retreat that day. When I came out I looked around and did not see our car so I thought I would walk over to the street. This way he would not have to pull into the parking lot and we could be on our way. I waited there about seven minutes or so. Then the idea came to me that I should start walking in the direction of the church. This way he could see me and I would be closer to church and get some exercise at the same time. I got to the top of the hill and he still had not come. He was probably talking to somebody, which was not unusual. But I was a little uneasy, something felt wrong. I continued to walk toward the church and finally arrived. No one was in the parking lot. I panicked. I ran into the church and there was a man there I knew. I explained that I had walked all the way there and Bob was probably looking for me at the store and could he please take me back to the store. Then I heard sirens blaring. I was sure that Bob thought I had been kidnapped and called the police. When we pulled up to the car, Bob looked horrified. "Where in the world have you been? I have been looking everywhere for you." The girls were crying and I was crying and we all were hysterical.

As I look back on that day I can laugh my self silly, but at the time, it was not funny at all. You would think I would not have been in such a rush, but sometimes we get in a rush when God wants us to wait. If I had just stayed put at the store and waited, there would not have been the confusion and I would not have had to walk up that hill. God did provide a way back to where I started from, and He will provide a way back to a fresh starting place every time. But wouldn't it be better just to wait for Him to pick us up and carry us instead of running ahead? We get ahead of God so many times, you would think that we would learn, but we don't. *"Wait for the Lord and He will save you."* Proverb 20:22b

Bob could not deny that his priority in life was God. He wanted to serve Him and could not get that out of his heart and mind. He searched the internet, and various other methods to find out what he could do in the ministry. He saw an ad in the paper that advertised for a minister in Gatlinburg, Tenn. for a wedding chapel. The ad gave a phone number and Bob called about it. It sounded interesting and would pay about six hundred dollars a week. So he filled out the application. They called him to come to Tennessee for an interview. It appealed to Bob, because on Sundays the chapel served as a church. Many people vacationed year around and they told us that part of the job would include a ministry to transit people in the area. Every Sunday Bob would preach and do weddings throughout the week. Gatlinburg was the wedding capital at that time and people came from all over to be married in the mountains at this beautiful resort area.

We prayed much about the job, but I was uneasy about it; however, I don't always have a handle on what God would have us to do. We had made several trips to Gatlinburg, and the folks wanted me to come and talk to them also. They said Bob and I would be working as a team. Not knowing what that meant, we had to sit down with the owner and talk about the possibilities available. When we got there they were busy trying to tell us how the business ran and how I would be booking weddings. They had me to sit down at the phones and talk to people as they called. I was to talk to them about the wedding packages. They said my responsibility would be to sell, sell, and sell. I did not like this idea at all. I was not a salesperson, and was not aware that I would be helping Bob at all until I went up there, and Bob was not either. We went to dinner with the owner and we discussed further arrangements, but his story began to change on the amount of pay Bob would be getting. It seemed that the six hundred dollars was for both of us working full time and that included Sundays, all holidays and weekends because that was when couples wanted to get married. That was their high volume days. We were already hired in one sense of the word, although I was extremely uncomfortable with this situation. Bob and I talked on the way home. He seemed excited, and although I was so uneasy, I did not say that I was. I did not want to discourage Bob if this was what he really wanted to do. After all who was I to question God about His plans for our lives?

The drive to Gatlinburg was so beautiful and we had gone several times to see if we could find a place to live. We asked the Lord that if He would have us to go, please give us a sign. We asked Him to sell our house. As we drove the "FOR SALE" sign into the hard ground, I was already questioning whether this was really what God wanted. Doubts filled my heart, but when the house sold in a couple days I thought it was just me and I had to make the adjustments required. I was concerned that I would be working so much the girls would have to raise themselves. This really disturbed me, but we were already committed. Bob had quit his job and was getting ready to move and I would go as soon as we could find a house.

Bob packed all his clothes and personal belongings, and left for Gatlinburg. I stayed behind and prepared to move. We had about thirty days before the closing on the house, but the couple purchasing our house was planning to be married and would not need it for a couple more months. Bob's mother came on several weekends to stay with the girls while I drove the better than four hour trip to be with Bob so we could be looking for housing. We just could not find anything we could afford. The realtor took us all over those mountains but there was always something not quite right with the house. Finally, we found one and put five hundred dollars down. It was not ideal, but it would do.

The next weekend I went up to be with Bob and work with him in the wedding chapel. It was sort of fun. I took pictures of the newly weds and we met lots of interesting and exciting people from all over. But something was just not quite right with the owner. The first time he paid Bob, he paid him in cash. There was no taxes taken out, there was no insurance, nothing. We did not know exactly how we felt about this but we were beginning to sense that this whole mess was sort-of underhanded. So when Bob told the owner that he would be going home for a few days to get things ready for the move, he took all his belongings back home. We loaded both cars and left.

As we talked and prayed and talked again we knew something was not right with this job. All weekend we were so restless and arranged a meeting with the pastor of our church. We told him of our suspicions and he said, "It sounds like you already know that this is not the right move for you guys right now." We knew that but I guess we just needed to hear someone else say what we already knew. The next day was Monday and Bob was going to call the owner of the wedding chapel, but before he had the chance to call, he called Bob. He told Bob that he had run into some trouble and that he was being arrested for tax evasion. He told us not to come back right now. Bob just said okay. It let us off the hook and we did not know if he was telling us the truth or not. Bob got his old job back at the restaurant equipment company and went back to work the next day.

Had we run ahead of God? I don't know if we did or not. But learning to wait on Him had been a trial in itself. We were in a dilemma now for sure. We had sold our house and had to find a place to live. We were getting desperate, or at least I was. One night I sat on the couch all night long and bawled so hard that I thought my heart would burst. I still could not bring myself to have the faith and trust that God was in control. Instead, here I was again floundering in self-pity and thinking this was the end of the road. I did not like the situation we were in. It made no sense to me that we had to struggle like this.

I did not know if I would ever get to the place that I could say that "I am completely trusting in You Lord." I was acting like God had sold the throne and moved out of heaven. I was overwhelmed with the burden I was trying to carry on my own. When would I ever learn to let God handle my life and quit worrying? I was so concerned about what others would say. I went back to Proverbs 3:5, & 6; for me trusting was very difficult. It was hard for me to relinquish everything to him. I was still acting like God did not know what He was doing. But how could I? Was I not a child of the King? Indeed I was but why was I still trying to control the situation by worrying. What would that accomplish? I knew it was getting me nowhere fast in this situation or in my spiritual life.

CHAPTER: XXIV

THE PIT

⌣∶∾

Isaiah 65:24 *And it shall come to pass that, before they call, I will answer; and while they are yet speaking, I will hear. (NKJV)*

We looked for some time and finally found a two story farm house in Winston-Salem which was our twenty-third place to live. The house was eighty years old and had a lot of problems, and was half finished on the second floor. A couple was splitting up and he had been remodeling the upstairs. We started looking for a house to rent but no one wanted to rent to a family with three children, two dogs and a cat so we knew our only option was to purchase. One realtor found a house for us but it was so tiny we would have been crawling over each other.

This old farm house was all we could afford. The bank told us they would not give us a loan on the house until the upstairs was finished. We got pre-approved for a loan and were able to move in and work on the house. Ross and Sarah helped us move so many times it became a joke. I know they got as tired of us moving as I was. As soon as we moved in I had a load of laundry to do. The washer water pumped out on the ground, which was illegal. The owner had told us the sewer lines for the washer was connected into the septic tank, but it wasn't. I called the realtor and they had to get in touch with the owner and have him to come connect the drain into the septic tank. He seemed to be deceptive on several other things as well so we knew he could not be trusted about anything he told us.

The bank gave us three months to finish the project. We had to complete the upstairs and then it would need inspecting again. Bob was working a lot of hours so that left little time to work on the house; we had evenings and Saturdays. Ross and Sarah came to our rescue and helped us. Alice Baker another friend came endless times and painted, scraped and sanded drywall. This project was a major undertaking and we really did not realize the amount of work it would take to get the walls mudded and ready to paint. We wallpapered the bathrooms, primed the walls and ceiling, built closets and painted. We all sanded until we thought our arms would fall off. But it was fun working together. It was a full-time job to have it completed for the final inspection. We do not know what we would have done without the help of our friends.

The inspectors came and the house passed final approval. Two weeks later we were in the lawyer's office ready to sign the papers for the closing. The owner had given power of attorney to the realtor to sign the papers so he did not come to the closing. We sat there quietly as the lawyer looked over the papers. All of the sudden he stopped and said, "OH NO! we have a problem here. The house behind your house is on your property." It took several more weeks to go back and straighten that problem out. The previous owner knew that the house was on their property, because it was his mother's house, but they said nothing. In fact her mother used to own the house we were purchasing. Finally the dilemma was resolved and we were able to sign the papers to the Brown House.

The house was very hot and we could not get it cooled. We had central air downstairs and nothing upstairs. The house was large and we later found out had no insulation. It cost us almost three hundred dollars in electric bills each month that fall. When it cooled down outside we noticed the house did not retain the heat from the day's sun. It cooled down as well at night.

The "Brown House" was a monster money pit. Something was breaking all the time, or needed repairs. We had four bathrooms and therefore four times the trouble with the old plumbing. The kitchen sink was constantly dripping so I got "Bob the Tool Man" to take a look to see if he could fix it. We had to purchase a new faucet, he said. When he went to put the new one on, we ended up having to replace the sink, and counter top. At one time the house had a coal stove in the dug out basement. The house had old vents in the floor so the heat would pass up into the rooms. Some one had boarded them up, but failed to brace them and I fell through one of them up to my waist. Kelly was running through the hall upstairs one night and rammed a splinter in her foot. We could not remove it so we ended up taking her to the hospital so they could get it out surgically.

Bob still was not making much money, only about three hundred a week. We were barely able to get the loan for the house and things were extremely tight. We had not anticipated the constant repairs and high cost of utilities in this house. There was no money for anything extra, especially with Christmas coming. I was way too proud to let my parents know of the financial situation we were in, so I never told them that we had no money to buy the girls anything for Christmas. Once again the Lord provided. A week before Christmas someone from our church called and asked what they could get the girls. I gave them a list of some things they would like to have. We had managed to get a tree and now there would be presents to go under it as well. Someone also had put an envelope in our mailbox with one hundred and sixty dollars in it. Now I could buy some groceries for a nice Christmas dinner. God had been so good to touch the hearts of His people once again. But I did not like the circumstances we were in. I was uncomfortable, embarrassed, and ashamed although no one knew of our financial situation. God was even using this circumstance somehow for my good even if I could not see past my pit.

> *"Though the Lord slay me, yet will I trust Him."* (Job 13:15)

How could I trust Him in all this? Was not God supposed to take care of us? Had I not given Him all? Or had I?

Joseph also had been cast into a pit. (Gen. 37:24) The pit was empty, dark and there was no water down there. A lot of times it felt like this was where I would stay. But just as sure as the Midianites lifted Joseph out of the pit, God lifted me out of the pit of discouragement and despair. Just as Joseph had told his brothers in Gen. 45:7 that God had sent him ahead to preserve their lives, God also prepares us in our circumstances. He was humbling me, preparing my heart to receive His will for my life. I felt like Joseph at times, that I had been forgotten. At times I felt the isolation of imprisonment locked in my own self. I was building a wall of protection around me, to keep the world from seeing the real me. I knew how it felt to be in a prison of one's own perspective. Satan will use anything to discourage us and to trap us in the pit of life. It is up to us if we get so discouraged that we fail to look up. He (The Lord) is our refuge, and our strength. He will lift us up out of the miry pit and set our feet on a solid foundation. (Psalm 40:2)

I knew that somehow I must help with the finances by getting a job. Kelly was going to school now so I could at least work part-time. I applied for a job as a church secretary. I went fifteen miles to make application and talk with the assistant pastor. Later they called me for the job and I was thrilled.

When I went to work the first morning the secretary proceeded to tell me that I was their last choice; everyone else had turned the job down because it was too far to drive. That really did not help my self esteem any. Somehow, I knew this was the job God had for me even if no one else would take it. I went in not knowing anything about the job or how to do the computer work, but I strived hard and taught myself the programs. We did not have a computer at home and I had never worked on one before, but I knew I was smart and a fast learner and I was determined to do a good job. I worked the afternoon shift from 11:00 a.m. to 4:00 p.m. As soon as I thought Kelly would be home I called her to make sure she was safe.

Brooke turned sixteen years old in April of 1995. She had been so sweet, but I had to watch her carefully. She was bent toward doing wrong and being as sneaky as she could to keep us from knowing what she was doing. She did not like Salem Academy and rebelled against doing any of her studies. One rule for our home was that the girls could not date until they were at least sixteen years old. As soon as Brooke turned sixteen, she came to us and said that the school was having a dance and she wanted to go, knowing that we would not approve. She begged and pleaded and we prayed and asked God what we should do. We wanted the girls to be responsible for the decisions they made in life so we told her we would leave it up to her if she promised she would seek God in this matter and do what He wanted her to do. We were astonished when she came back the following day and said that God told her that it was okay for her to go. As I look back, it was one of the biggest mistakes we made with Brooke. We had prayed and hoped that she would come to the conclusion that it would be wrong for a Christian to go to a dance. She would be with so many unsaved people, and we knew how impressionable Brooke was. It was against our wishes but we allowed her to go.

While she was there she met a boy who was in Hardgrave Military Academy. We were somewhat impressed with him going to the military academy and all, but he called Brooke and wanted to take her out. She was sixteen now, but we were not ready for this. We told Brooke that he would need to spend some time with us before she went out with him. When he came to pick her up he was very respectful and polite. I had fixed lunch and we sat out on the deck to eat and chat. One could say he made a good first impression and they continued to date when he came into town to visit his family, although we really did not have good feelings about this guy.

In January of 1996 my folks left for Florida. Later that month we had a horrible sleet storm that lasted for twenty-four hours. We were without power and it was so cold in the house. Mandy and Brooke went to spend the night with some of their friends. We were able to keep warm by a kerosene heater, and ate the best way we could. Kelly stayed home with us. We were without power for three days and when it did come back on we had no heat. The motor for the fan went out on the furnace. It took two more days to get that fixed. My parents could not believe that it was so cold here and so nice in Florida.

I needed a full time job so we could have some insurance. Bob's diabetes had come back and we could not afford an individual policy. I applied for assistant director of a day care our church was opening and got the job. I loved it from the very beginning. The children were so sweet and I did enjoy being with them. My responsibilities started out with doing the bookkeeping and payroll for the day care. I tried my best to be very conscientious about every detail so as not to make mistakes.

Mother and dad came home Friday evening, March 25. Mother had called us from Florida and said dad had been having chest pains, but we did not know how bad it was until they got home. Dad drove all the way home in one day. He was afraid he would get worse and did not want to be out of town when it happened. Mother said that dad had taken about a hundred nitroglycerines tablets that week to stay out of pain as much as possible. We went over to their house to see them about an hour after they arrived. Dad seemed to be calm and said not to worry, that he would be fine. Mother took dad to the hospital later that night.

The doctor admitted him and test revealed that all four of the bypasses they had done twelve years previously were closed off and he would have to stay on a nitroglycerin drip until they could do surgery. The following Thursday surgery was scheduled and we all gathered in my dad's room before 7:00 a.m. Dad was so worried about the surgery and kept trying to figure out what the doctors were going to do to improve his condition. I said, "Daddy, I just got to know, are you sure you are saved?"

He emphatically said, "Yes, I know I am!" I just had to ask him although he had claimed to be a Christian since I was a child. However, there were numerous times that I questioned his faith. Dad had not grown much as a Christian and sometimes I doubted his salvation. On several occasions he made ugly remarks about things, such as "I don't have time to go to church; I have to work for a living". I knew that was an insult to us since we had been out of public work, being missionaries.

Shortly the nurse came and took dad to surgery. As she rolled him away she said, "I have your chariot awaiting you, Mr. Jestes." I remembered that so well because I thought of Elijah taking his chariot to heaven and wondered if this would be dad's chariot that would usher him into the presence of God.

The doctor told us this would be a very long and complicated operation. When nine hours passed before he was put into recovery we expected as much. The doctor came out and told us that dad had a very hard time and that he was on a heart/lung machine and that it was doing all the work for him. He said we could go back and see him in recovery. My mother kept saying, "Something is not right." She kept saying that over and over. She was referring to the tube they had inserted into his mouth but it was not taped as mother had remembered it should have been. I felt of him and he was so very cold. But they said he was okay and it would be touch and go. After I saw dad, I went home, but first I needed to stop and pick up some stuff at the grocery store. When I arrived home, Bob said my mother had called and dad had died. We rushed back to the hospital. I could not believe that my dad was gone. The man who often kissed me on the back of my neck and hugged me so tight was never to hug me again. O death you are so cruel. But thanks be to God, He gives us the victory over death.

It was the week before Easter Sunday and I had to sing in the cantata and Bob was the narrator. We did manage to participate in the program after the funeral but it was hard to fight back the emotions. I wanted to sing, because God had given me something to sing about. I knew that one day I would see my heavenly Father and my dad would be there waiting for us. I was sad, but I could not be sad for my dad, because I knew that he was in the presence of the one who provided the reason behind Easter. He took our shame, our sin and our punishment so that we also might live with Him. Because He lives I could face another day.

My mom had a horrible time adjusting. She stayed with my sister for a month before she could go back home. A part of her died the day my father died. She grieved so much for him; it hurt me to see her in so much pain. Her desire was to die as well, but God was not ready for her yet. She had work to do, here. She became active in her church and began to interact with the other widows. She reached out to others who were hurting with pain and afflictions. I saw her cry so often and she confided that she wished she could die as well, that life had no meaning now that dad was gone.

In October of that year the director of the day care gave her notice and took another job that offered maternity benefits. From November until March, I worked ten hours a day managing the day care. I knew there was a job that had to be done and somebody had to do it. In March the chairman of the board brought a lady down and said she was to be the new director.

She came in and started ordering me around. Things got touchy but soon it was discovered that she had lied on her resume about a previous job at another day care. She had been fired from that job after she had ran the assistant director off. The chairman of the day care arranged for her departure.

Again, I managed the day care until they appointed another employee to take the job. It worked out great though. She worked from 8:00 a.m. until 3:00 p.m. and most of the time was off on Fridays. She was so easy to get along with and I quickly found out that she allowed me run the day care. At this point I was doing the payroll and taxes, all the ordering of supplies and making most of the decisions. I handled registration, parents, and employees as well as cooking on occasion when needed. Things were going pretty good until she took another position a year and a half later. Once again I was placed in interim position. They appointed another girl with an associate's degree. She lasted one week. Again, they asked me to serve as interim director. This time it was for a very long interim, about one year.

Mandy had graduated from Salem Academy in May '95 and decided to take some time off from studies so she worked in the day care as one of the teachers. By spring of 1996 she had enough of pre-school and decided to get a French degree at University of North Carolina at Greensboro. She entered in the fall semester of 1996 and commuted the thirty mile drive. I was trusting God every day that she would be safe in the traffic. She drove a tiny car and I knew if a truck hit her, she would be history. We decided that it would be better if she could move to Greensboro so she would have more time for her studies and not have to travel back and forth on that bad interstate. My mother and I helped her move into a room in preparation for the fall 1997 semester. Mandy had done very well at Salem Academy in French. She had won third place on the National French Exam in the State of North Carolina. She was excellent in language studies. She had taken Latin, Greek, Hebrew, and spoke fluent French and Italian, oh, and of course English.

Brooke had been giving us a hard time over the guy she had met at the dance she attended at Salem Academy. Since then, she had quit Salem and decided to attend another public high School, but he influenced her to quit school. He had dropped out of the military academy and moved back home with his mother and sister, but he did finish high school. I knew that Brooke was with the wrong people and that she was up to no good. She lied to us about everything she was asked about, but at the time we could not see that. She was a convincing liar. She had started smoking and at the time we did not know it but she was on pot as well.

June of 1997 Brooke ran away to Florida with Mike. She had just turned eighteen in April and there was nothing we could do about it except go get the car that she took. We knew that if we didn't it would be destroyed. I just knew that God was going to take care of her, somehow. When the girls were dedicated to the Lord, we asked Him to take them if they would grow up to deny Him and end up shaming God and go to Hell. We gave them over to God and thanked Him for allowing us to have them for a while. We knew they ultimately belonged to Him. I had a peace that God would protect Brooke. I did not like it, and I was upset to say the least. We prayed constantly for her safety and asked God to bring her back home where she belonged. Oh my little prodigal! How long will you rebel against us and God?

This was one situation I could do nothing about. I could not control Brooke and I could not make her do anything she did not want to do or make her do the things I thought best for her. Little by little I began to see that God was the one in control, not me. I began to acknowledge that I no longer wanted to have control over this problem or any other. I did not need that responsibility and was tired of trying to be in control of everything. I relinquished my desires to God and I began to realize that I had always worn myself out trying to take on the responsibilities God never intended for me to have. I quit worrying about every little problem, and I did not worry about Brooke. I knew God would take care of her, she was His.

Brooke called on occasion, when she needed money, or food. But we would not send her any money because we knew it would be misused for drugs or something foolish. I would send her groceries instead and asked her to call me when they arrived so I would know that she got them.

She went to Florida with the idea she was going to make a lot of money, but once there she found out that was not the case. They could hardly keep their heads above water. I had suspected from what Mandy told me that they were taking drugs often.

In February of the next year (1998) Brooke called me at work in the afternoon and said she had not eaten in three days and she had no food or money. If you do not think that makes a Mother's heart break, you are sadly mistaken. I rushed out and bought her some food items and ran as fast as I could to UPS before they sent the last shipment to Florida. It was costly to overnight the package but I still could not see sending money. I made it just in time and they said it would be there by mid-morning. On the way home, right about 7:30 p.m. I prayed, "Oh, dear God, You know my heart and how it is breaking for my child and I know your heart is far more grieved for Brooke than I can imagine. I know that you love her more than I can ever love her. But Lord if you would please send someone into her life to buy her something to eat, I would be grateful."

The next morning, Brooke called about 10:00 a.m. and said the package arrived and thanked me for it. I asked her if she was ready to come home yet and she said she wasn't. Then she told me that her boss at a restaurant where she worked bought her supper last night. I asked her what time did she have supper and she said about 7:30 p.m.

Does God ever amaze you? Well He shouldn't. Because He is waiting to do exceedingly more than we can ask or think. I don't know why we are surprised when God answers our prayers. He answers all our prayers, just not in the way we expect nor in the way we would like for Him to answer. I know one time when we were on deputation we were coming back from a trip to Pennsylvania. We had to cross the Chesapeake Bay Bridge and Tunnel but Bob did not want to cross it that rainy night. It was a holiday and every motel we stopped at was full. We asked the Lord to help us find a room that night so we would not have to cross the bridge. The last motel before the bridge had one room left. There was a couple behind us ready to take the room if we did not want it, but we did not ask God for a reasonable rate and the motel room cost us around one hundred dollars. That was expensive in 1978. We learned to be more specific in our prayers after that.

Kelly was an amazing child. She never complained about all the time and attention I had spent at work and the problems we had with Brooke. Little did I know how all this was impacting her life. She began to see so many mistakes

Brooke was making and she determined in her heart that she would not make the same mistakes.

CHAPTER: XXV

A SHOT IN THE DARK
⌣∶∿

Psalms 91:11 *For he shall give his angels charge over thee, to keep thee in all thy ways.*

We always made it a point to pray each day for our girls. Our prayer would be for them to give the Lord first place in their hearts. We just were not sure whether Mandy had done that or not. She had strong convictions and she was a strong believer but we did not believe she was going in the right direction for her life. One night after she had started the 1997 fall semester at about 3:00 a.m. the phone rang and it was the voice of a very scared child; our child, Mandy. She began to unravel her story.

Someone came to her door about 10:00 p.m. It was a guy and two girls. Their tale was that the guy needed to go upstairs to a friend's apartment to fix things up for a surprise party, and wanted to know if the girls could remain with Mandy. These people were complete strangers she had never seen before. She did not suspect any foul play so she said okay. After several hours Mandy was wondering what was going on, because the two girls were still at her place. They seemed to have a lot in common. Mandy had a guitar and one of the girls played. That seemed to bond them together. One of the girls was the mother of a baby, which was left at home. She kept saying that she needed to get home to the baby. Finally, the guy came back and the mother said that she needed to go home, so the guy asked Mandy if she could take the girl home so she could take care of her baby. Mandy said she would. The guy and the other girl insisted that Mandy follow them, but they needed to go by an ATM machine first. After they had stopped at about three ATM machines and got money at each machine, they finally arrived at some houses in the projects. The girl that was with the guy got out of the car and went in a house and came back out with something tucked in the front of her jeans. Later Mandy found out that it was a gun. They left and went a few more blocks and the boy and girl in the car behind Mandy got out and they were arguing very loudly. He then went into a house. The girl walked up to Mandy's car. She asked "So how long have you known this guy and how do you know him?" Mandy told her that she had never seen this guy before. By this time Mandy was getting scared. Why was she asked to take the girl home when they ended up following her? The girl got mad because she said that the guy told her that Mandy owed him money for drugs. When he came out of the house the girls said "You lied to us." The guy took off running, she pulled the gun out of her jeans, shot at him and hit him in the shoulder. Mandy said she heard the bullet fly past her ear. She jumped back into her car. The two girls got into Mandy's back seat and told her to drive. She told her where to drop her off and told Mandy how to get back home.

As soon as she got home she called us and wanted to know what she should do, so Bob told her to call her cousin Ryan, which was a police officer. He told her that he was sending a car over to her house to get her story, and told her not to open the door. Shortly there was a knock at the door and she presumed it was the police and opened the door to see the two girls standing there. They were looking for the guy that was shot. Mandy was afraid they were coming after her, and she told them that the police would be there any minute and they better leave. When the officer came, he took her story, but told Ryan that he thought Mandy was in on the shooting, that it appeared like a drug deal gone bad. Ryan just laughed and said, "Man you are way off base. Mandy is a missionary's kid and she does not even know her way around Greensboro. She does not take drugs either." The police officer could not be easily convinced. He was sure she was in on a drug deal.

The guy that was shot recovered, but Mandy had to go to court later to tell her side of the story. She became aware that this world is not as safe as she had thought and as she grew up thinking. Italy was a much different place. She had been sheltered from all the violence in our society and she really did not believe anything like this could occur to her. God began to use that experience in her life. She was ready to listen and follow Him above all else. She told us that she wanted to attend a Christian College and made plans to attend Cincinnati Bible College in the fall (1998).

Right about the same time, Brooke called and had decided that she needed to come home. I told her to pack her things and I would be there the next day to pick her up. Mandy and I left very early the next morning and drove to Florida. When we got there to pick Brooke up she wanted to know if I would bring Mike back and I said that I would not. I said, "He got down here on his own and he can get back the best way he can." Mike's uncle was a rich doctor and not married. He constantly was bailing Mike out of trouble and this time would be no exception.

After we picked Brooke up, we drove about three hours back and were pulled over by a Highway Patrolman. I was driving but I was not speeding. I did not know why I was being stopped. The officer came to the car and asked if I wanted something. I didn't know what he was talking about.

He said that I was flashing my lights, was something wrong? I said, "Oh, no sir, I am sorry. My alternator is going to the bad and the lights keep dimming. He said I ought to stop for the night. I had planned to drive straight back but we all were tired, it was late and the lights on the car weren't working properly. Mike was home in a couple days and was already contacting Brooke. We did not want her to see Mike again, but we realized that this was a hopeless request.

When I picked Brooke up in Florida she was so skinny and seemed angry. She also was high on something. She said she was forced to come home because they had no money for food, rent or any thing else. She did not want to come back. She had really changed, and not for the better. She was rebellious, bitter and angry.

Mike had abandoned his car, as it was ready for the junk yard. We had kept Brooke's car for her for when she returned. Mike had a hold on Brooke we could not deny. He controlled her every thought and action.

Mike's uncle insisted they attend the church he attended shortly after they got home. We did not care as long as she was hearing the gospel. After a couple of weeks Brooke came to us and said she had made a big mistake and that she wanted to get her life right with the Lord and us. We were praising God that she was ready to make some changes. She and Mike were wanting to get married.

In July Brooke and Mike were married. I had high hopes that it would work out, but there was still something about him that I just could not trust. He had apologized to us for influencing Brooke to go to Florida, but in my book, I could not trust him although he had said he had accepted Christ as his Savior and that was a changed person.

In August we took Amanda to Cincinnati. She had sold her car and was going to live on campus and give herself wholeheartedly to the Lord and her studies. It was very difficult for me as I left my first-born so very far away. I cried all the way back home. Things were very different around our house. There were only three of us now, except for the same two dogs and the same cat. Now was the time to think about downsizing our house a bit. The big "Brown House" had consumed too much money, but now we could live in a smaller place because we no longer had Brooke and Mandy at home. We sold the house in a short time and moved to a rent house on Anderson Drive in the fall of 1998. This was our twenty-fourth home in the twenty-three years of marriage.

Bob had been happy serving the Lord in an eldership capacity, and taught several classes at church we were now attending. He began to search the possibility of going into full time ministry as a pastor. In the spring of 1999 a church in Kentucky wanted him to come out to candidate for the pastorate, so we planned a trip and went. We did not tell anyone what we were going for, but when we returned a couple of the elders told Bob not to make any decisions right away. We do not know how they found out anything. Within a couple of months they had talked to Bob and offered him a position at our church as Senior Adult Minister and Pastoral Care. It was a tremendous blessing, an answer to our prayers and Bob's life long desire had finally been fulfilled. November 1999 Bob took the position and left the restaurant equipment business. We have felt so blessed to be a part of the Ministry of Pinedale Christian Church. Bob is so happy doing what he has wanted to do for a lifetime, serving the Lord. The church is growing and God is blessing lives.

We lived on Anderson Drive one year. After Bob was hired by the church, we were able to purchase another home. Once again we were so amazed at all the details the Lord worked out for us. Kelly was so excited she wanted to put the Christmas tree up before we moved in; and we did. We moved in our twenty-fifth home one week after Thanksgiving.

In the fall of 1999 Mandy had transferred colleges. She felt led to go to South Eastern Theological Bible College in Wake Forest, North Carolina to finish her degree there. I was glad to have her home for the summer. We had packed her a few things and she moved into an apartment with some other girls just two hours away. Wake Forest was a small town, rather pretty, just on the northern side of Raleigh. She seemed to like living there and found a job in a coffee shop to help with her expenses.

She met a guy and I could tell that Mandy really liked him. She was such a private individual and never wanted "mommy" to find out anything about her, but I could tell by the way she talked about this guy that she loved him; however he had a hard time committing. Sounded all too familiar to me. I advised Mandy to forget him and focus on her studies and find someone else. She said she thought that would be best.

In II Corinthians 1:3 it talks about our God of all comfort, comforted us in times of trouble and we can in turn comfort others going through the same things. We could share in each other's sufferings and we could also share in each other's comfort. I was able to help Mandy see that some people have a problem with making commitments. Or that maybe this was just not the right person for her. She was hurt because he did not feel the same way about her that she felt for him. Oh how I understood that from experience. God had allowed me to go through the same thing so that twenty-six years later I could help my own child with the same feelings that I had. The trial I had gone through had not been in vain after all, and that is the way we have to look at every tribulation, every test of faith and every disappointment.

God does not afflict us with pain, but we do walk though this life with many things that occur that is not to our liking. "It rains on the just and on the unjust." (Matthew 5:45) Just because we are Christians does not make us immune to pain and sufferings. *"We do not want you to be uninformed, brothers, about the hardships we suffered.....We were under great pressure, far beyond our ability to endure so that we despaired of life. Indeed, in our hearts we felt the sentence of death. But this happened that we might not rely on ourselves but on God, who raises the dead. He has delivered us from such a deadly peril, and he will deliver us. On him we have set our hope that he will continue to deliver us."* (II Cor. 1 8-10)

Brooke and Mike had problem after problem and got to the point they had no where to turn. They moved into our basement and set up a small area for living where they lived for a year. Mike still could not be trusted in my book. One time he accused Kelly of stealing money in their bedroom which was Brooke's. It was about three hundred dollars. I was so upset that he had accused her. She would never even go into their living space the entire time they stayed in our home. Brooke felt she had to cover for him, since he was her husband. Finally, Mike decided he was going to go to school in Wilmington, and his uncle paid for everything for them to move. I felt in my heart that Brooke was truly not happy. She often cried and seemed so depressed, but who wouldn't be. Mike was a selfish child who needed to take some responsibility for his life.

In August of 2001 they packed their things, and moved to Wilmington. Mike entered the Coast Guard School and for once I thought (maybe it was hope) that this would work out after all. I seldom heard from Brooke so I really did not know how things were going. Sometime later my mom and sister and I took a girls weekend and went down to spend some time with Brooke. It was so much fun being together just the four of us. We would get silly and laugh so hard at ourselves. Brooke seemed to enjoy our trip down to see her. I sensed she was depressed with her situation. Only a mother knows when her child is hurting although no words are ever spoken. After a long walk on the beach she began to tell me just a little bit of what she was going through. I begged Brooke to seek the Lord about what she should do.

She never revealed how Mike was really treating her and it was not until she left him a year later that she began to unravel the details to me of how he was abusing her and how he was drinking and using drugs. One day he finally went too far and scared Brooke and she did not feel safe with him any longer. She moved in with a friend for a couple of weeks until she found a place to live.

Bob and I took some furniture down for her apartment. Brooke looked happy for the first time in the four years she had been married. We realized she had been living in a difficult situation. Mike had verbally abused Brooke for years without our knowing, all along while she had covered up for him and tried to hide so much from us. Why? Well, she had begun to believe his lies of how we did not care for her and how she was no good and worthless. He had convinced her that no one loved her and she was not worthy of love.

Doesn't the devil himself tell those lies and people believe him as well. He convinces people that God does not love them and can not because their sins are so bad. He tells them that God will not forgive them because they do not deserve to be forgiven. It does not take too much for people to believe those lies. At that point the devil has them wrapped around his finger and they feel hopeless and lost.

In April 2003, Mandy told us she had met someone on the internet in January and they had a lot in common. I did not think too much about it, until she said after she graduated in May she might go to California. I asked her how she planned to go since she had no money and no job on the west coast. She said she would get a transfer with Borders the company where she was employed. I just dismissed the thought and in May she announced that the guy she had been conversing with lived in California and that he was going to fly here and they were going to get married. Well, I could not really believe that. How could someone marry another person they had never met before? She kept talking about this, saying it was really going to occur, but we just did not believe that she could do something like that. I kept begging her not to be serious about such a thing. Surely she could not go through with this plan. What about getting to know him and what if he was a pervert or something?

We were so proud of Amanda when she graduated from college. It had taken her seven years from the time she started since she had changed colleges and majors a couple times. It was a beautiful sunny morning when many gathered for the graduation ceremony. The trees were blooming and the birds were singing as the graduates lined up to receive their well earned diplomas. Afterwards we took Mandy out to lunch to celebrate. My mother was so excited to see her graduate. This was her only grandchild that had graduated from college.

Mandy remained in Wake Forest after graduation. She said that she planned to live there until the end of July. She kept saying she was going to get married and that she would stay there until she left to go to California, but I had no reason to believe she was getting married. We had not even talked to the guy she told us about. I knew Mandy was not a liar, but I thought that some man was just leading her on.

On June 28, we had planned to meet Ross and Sarah and go out to eat for our anniversaries. We had not been out with them in a while. Mandy called and said she wanted to come home for a visit. This was highly unusual for her to call and say she wanted to come home for such a short time. I told her that we were getting ready to go out with Ross and Sarah and she could meet us for supper. She said, "No, I can't stay long. I just wanted to come home so you could meet my husband." You could have knocked me over with a feather. I was in shock to say the least. Bob kept saying "Now Jane don't be upset, you know Mandy kept saying this is what she was going to do for a long time." How could I not be upset, I did not even know this guy's last name.

And she actually did it. Daniel flew in from California on June 26th and they went to the Justice of the Peace and got married. On June 30th he flew back to California, and Mandy packed up and joined him on August 2nd. To this day it is still inconceivable to me how she could have done this. She kept telling me that pre-arranged marriages go on all the time around the world. "Mom, you don't have to meet them first. It will be okay, I promise. Just wait and see Daniel is a nice guy." She tried to convince me, but I was in shock. They had talked extensively over the phone and they felt they knew each other well enough to make this decision.

Kelly was now fifteen years old and was an ideal child in so many ways. She was attending a Christian school and was doing well. She was a blessing to us as well as to my mom who adored her, but after my dad had passed away it was hard for Kelly to adjust to being around my mom. She withdrew from her and my mom could not understand why. I knew that she was just growing up and she was changing and did not want to be around older people as much as she did her friends. I also think a large part of it had to do with her dealing with Billy's and my dad's death.

CHAPTER XXVI

THE BIG MISTAKE

✌∴∾

I Peter 1:7 *That the trial of your faith, being much more precious than of gold that perisheth, though it be tried with fire, might be found unto praise and honor and glory at the appearing of Jesus Christ,*

My mother and sister and her husband were planning a trip out west. They said they were going as far as California, so I asked them, if I flew out there could I stay with them in their motor home and visit Mandy. Soon the day arrived and in June of 2004, I flew to Los Angeles to surprise Mandy for her birthday. I had only seen Dan for about twenty minutes up until then and I knew nothing about him. Getting to know my son-in-law was great. He was warm, friendly, kind and seemed to love Amanda very much. They had been married almost a year now and I missed Mandy so much.

California was surprisingly nice. Hollywood was nothing like I imagined. It was rather a plain little town with all kinds of shops and the only extraordinary thing I witnessed was the stars on the sidewalk.

Bob and I began to pray that Daniel would seek other employment and get out of Hollywood. We did want them closer to us, but anywhere would have been okay. It was not long before Mandy communicated to us that Daniel was very unhappy in his work. The following year they moved to North Carolina and Mandy worked in the day care at our church once again, while Daniel built his business. He was a free-lance publicist.

In the fall of 2005 we had a singing group to come to our church. As the young woman stood before us she gave her testimony that she was raised in a Christian home and that her dad always told her that "**GOD MAKES NO MISTAKES**". She said she wrestled with that often, but when she would come home from school and things did not go right, her dad would tell her "Don't worry honey; God is in Control, HE MAKES NO MISTAKES". She said she never fully understood the essence of that until one day her father passed away. He had been in a wheel chair for some time after having his legs amputated from complications of diabetes. She said she could hear him say, "Don't worry honey, God makes no mistakes". She said she finally understood that God makes no mistakes, no matter what happened.

I really grasped those four little words. I didn't know why it was so profound to me, but those words, "GOD MAKES NO MISTAKES" was stamped on my heart forever. I would forget that phrase and would ask Bob again, "What was it that girl said?" and he would once again tell me, "God Makes No Mistakes!" Finally I wrote it down on a scratch pad and put it on the refrigerator. I looked at it every day and thought to myself, "Wow that is so great!" I did not know why those four words were so special at the time but they were like drops of water for my thirsty soul. Why did I attach myself to what that girl said? Why did such a simple statement I had heard all my life make such an impact on me now? It was like pure honey from God's throne. I could not go a day without dwelling on those words. They were sweet, they were profound, they were reassuring, and they brought peace to my soul.

Four weeks later is when I made the biggest mistake anyone could make. I had told an employee from the day care which had been there only a month that I could not use them anymore, because the parents were complaining. I failed to use proper terminology and did not seek direction from my superior and for eight months I had to suffer the burden of my mistake, while all along God was telling me "I MAKE NO MISTAKES" I had made a bad mistake. For a while I thought everything would work out, but to my dismay the complaint at the Equal Employment Opportunity turned against me. They had insisted I was trying to cover-up the truth, but I had not lied. For eight months I had held onto God's promise that He made no mistakes. This person claimed to be a Christian, why was he doing this? Did he not know what the Bible said about taking another Christian to court? Everything was so hard for me to comprehend and understand why all this was happening. I kept blaming myself.

Things were difficult and Bob's mother had been diagnosed with bone cancer. She was ninety years old and had suffered several operations and two broken hips, now she was at the point of death. On March 9 they had called for us to come to the nursing home, she would not make it much longer. All night we held her hand and prayed with her. Moments slipped away into hours and she had been unresponsive for sometime. Her breathing became worse and every breath seemed like her last. Finally at about 9:15 p.m. on March 10, Ruth was taken by God's precious angels and ushered into heaven as all four children gathered with their families around her. She drew her last breath, her heart stopped. She slipped her hands from mine and lifted them toward heaven then dropped them. As we gathered around Ruth's body sobbing, Bob led in prayer, thanking God for this Godly woman who gave so much of herself to others.

He asked for comfort for all of us and wisdom for the days ahead.

I had never seen anyone die before. Later I asked Bob was this usual for one to raise their hands upward as if to grasp an unseen vision and he said he had never seen anyone do that before. Death seems frightening but it is something not to be feared by the Christian. God has already defeated death so that we will not see death as some may know it. *"by his death he might destroy him who holds the power of death— that is the devil—and free those who all their lives were held in slavery by their fear of death"* Hebrews 2:14-15

After the funeral I returned to work on Monday. My supervisor came and asked to see me and Bob together. There in my husband's office I was asked if I would resign my job. I was devastated. I began to question God, but those words flew into my face again, "God makes no mistakes". How could I trust that anymore? This seemed worse that death itself. How could I face myself, my family my friends. I wanted to crawl into a hole and pull the dirt over my head. I did not care if I every saw the light of another day. I was angry, embarrassed and most of all hurt. How could I ever get over this terrible thing?

Much of my life had been like this. The very things that feel as if they were the end of me are only the beginning of something that God is trying to teach me. God was with me and assured me of his presence in visible ways although I was in anguish. I could not understand why God had allowed me to make such a stupid mistake. All I could think of was what was to become of us now? We were always one paycheck away from broke. Kelly was in college and we were still paying for Mandy's education. But somehow I rested in those words I grasped so tightly, "God makes no mistakes" I spent countless hours crying, praying and seeking God's wisdom in all this. I gave a two months notice and my last day would be May 25th.

My mother was also devastated when I broke the news to her. She worried night and day herself how we were going to keep Kelly in college. She questioned me constantly about how we were going to be able to make it. I told her that God had not let us down yet and that he would provide, just like He had always provided in the past. He had brought us to this time in our lives, not to harm us but to grow us. She had a hard time trying to understand how I could have been asked to leave. I tried to assure her that we would be fine while I was also struggling with those same issues.

Bob and I were desperate to try to understand what we should do financially. We looked at condominiums, thinking we might have to sell the house. We did not know how we were going to be able to make the house payments, two car payments, utilities, healthcare, insurance, keep Kelly in college and buy groceries. We sat down and prayed about what to do. Bob said he thought we might be able to make it but it would be very tight until I could find another job. We had always lived by faith and God had brought us this far. He could certainly provide for us now.

I get so tired of the battles in life. We hardly get one trial under our belts when another one seems to appear. However, now I view trials and problems as growth opportunities and it gives me a chance to see how God is going to work in and through me. It took me some time but I realized that God was interested in perfecting the distinctive qualities of my life and He was not interested in my comfort. Once again I was on the operation table. I did not like it and I was tired of being crushed. I wanted to scream, "Not fair at all God!" I am sure I did. I would suffer big time for this event, not only financially but personally in many ways.

The Holy Spirit gave me comfort and I worked for the remaining two months without anyone knowing what was transpiring behind the scenes. Often I prayed, "God this is not fair, I told the truth and the person trying to gain from this is wrong, but I am going to trust you no matter what in realizing that you love me and that you make no mistakes." I tried desperately to convince my mother that I was fine and that we were going to make it. However she continued to struggle with worry. She cried and felt the pain I felt. Moms are just like that you know no matter how old you get.

Mandy and Daniel were not happy living in North Carolina. They had taken a trip to Salem, Massachusetts to survey the possibility of moving there the first of July. It worked out that she gave her two week notice and was out of the day care the same time I left.

Bob was leaving for a mission's trip on May 30th. He was going to Italy for a pastor's convention where he would be preaching and doing some training. I wondered what I would do while he was gone perhaps my mother and I could do some things together. We talked of going on a vacation to the beach to see my sister while he was gone but I really was not much in the mood. I told her we would talk about it later.

CHAPTER XXVII

GOD MAKES NO MISTAKES

Revelation 21:4 *And God shall wipe away all tears from their eyes; and there shall be no more death, neither sorrow, nor crying, neither shall there be any more pain; for the former things are passed away.*

My little blessing, Kelly, was turning into a wonderful young woman. God had brought abundant blessings into our lives through her and He has blessed her beyond measure as well. She has been an amazingly great child. She said she had seen so many girls make mistakes, not excluding her sisters, and she did not want to mess up her life with stupid decisions. She has been so wise and mature for her age.

Kelly was very distraught when I told her of losing my job. She was working and going to college at the University of North Carolina at Charlotte. The ice cream shop did not pay very well although she worked as many hours as possible. She asked me on several occasions what would happen about college since I was not going to be working now. I told her I would try to find a job as soon as I could. This time we could not go in debt for college. At our age there would be no way we could get a loan paid off before retirement age. Somehow, I just did not have it in me yet to go job searching. What if I made another mistake? People do make mistakes you know. How could I survive another failure? I had a difficult time forgiving myself for the stupid mistake I had made. I felt I had disappointed God, myself, Bob and my family.

Kelly did not like her job in the ice cream shop at all. She was around young adolescents that were disrespectful and cursed. That disturbed her often. She had to work very late, sometimes getting home at 2:00 a.m. in the morning. One Saturday morning she called me and said, "Mom, could you please pray for me to get another job. I really need to find something else to do; this job is driving me crazy." I told her I would. Kelly was a delightful child to raise and she had so much going for her. She was nineteen years old and had a great head on her shoulders. I could not have asked for a better child. I did pray for her that day like I do each and every day, but asked God especially to provide a better job for her.

I had hired Kelly to work at the day care when she was sixteen. She really did not want to go to work, but I needed the help and she needed to learn to work. I was pretty tough on all my girls when they worked for me at the day care. They had to work harder because I expected more from them than I did the other employees. I did not let them get away with calling in sick either. Kelly was a very hard worker and she learned a lot of responsibility working at the day care. She would help me off the clock and even come in when she was not scheduled if I was short of workers. All this she did without complaining about her measly six dollars an hour job. She worked there a year and a half before I raised her to seven dollars an hour. Kelly was worth much more than some of the others employees that made eight and nine dollars an hour. I had taught her how to be a good employee and to be a responsible person.

That night Kelly called and she was so excited. "Oh, mother," she exclaimed. "This lady came into the ice cream shop tonight and offered me a job."

"Tell me about what happened Kelly." I said.

"Well, I can't talk long mom, I am on my break, but this lady came in and asked for me, I was in the back, and I came out and she said, 'Do you remember me, I was in here last week?' And I told her I did. She said she 'was so impressed with my customer service' that she wanted me to come to work at the hospital for her." Kelly was so excited that God had answered prayer and I was quite amazed myself.

Finally the day arrived and I prepared for the graduation ceremony at the day care. This was to be my last day and no one knew. I had wanted to work until the pre-school children had graduated. The children were so excited about the event that evening. We had twenty-six boys and girls leaving the day care going to kindergarten. Their parents were very proud of them as they recited what they had learned. I had made it a point for our day care not to be a babysitting service but a learning facility. We offered a great service for our community and the schools around the area really appreciated what we had taught the children. They were not only smart but they were ready for school and they knew what was expected of them.

After graduation I told my assistant with tears in my eyes that this was my last day of work that I had been asked to resign. We cried together as I finished packing my office and left her my keys. Again tears filled my eyes as I walked to my car that evening, looking around at the parents as they waved good-by, not knowing this would be the last time they would see me. I loved that day care, it was my ministry, and this was another mission field that burdened my tender heart for the lost. I had so many opportunities to share the love of God and had seen people come to church and get their lives in line with God's word. I drove slowly on the way home as

I kept saying, "God, I am trusting you because you make no mistakes. I don't understand and I certainly do not like this." I was angry, not with God, but with all that had brought me to this point.

On Friday the 26th of May, my first official day unemployed, the first thing I did was to fix my mother's hair that morning. She always wanted me to do her hair because I was the only one who knew how she wanted it to look. Full bangs as far down as I could get them since she had an extremely high forehead. Mother did not say a lot, she seemed very quite, distant to some measure. Once again she brought the subject of how we were going to keep Kelly in college. I told her I had no answers right then and changed the subject. She was pleased to hear that she would be going for an interview at the hospital.

She complained about her neck hurting on the right side. She had had a bad infection in her right ear lobe and just finished her antibiotic. After I finished her hair she stood up and gave me a big hug for a long time and told me that she loved me as we embraced. I told her that I loved her as well. I could tell she was not feeling too well. She had been diagnosed with COPD (Chronic Obstructive Pulmonary Disease) almost a year earlier and was short of breath at times. There were about four or five times in the past year she had been to the emergency room because she could not breathe. She had told us that she had quit smoking like the doctor had suggested. Mom had smoked for about sixty years. "I can't believe I have done this to myself." she would say.

The rest of Friday was very busy trying to arrange finances and making sure things were ready for Bob to leave on Tuesday. We had gone out to eat with our friends Ross and Sarah and had gotten home rather late, about 10:00 p.m. I had a message on the answer machine from my mother.

"Call me if you get in before I go to bed at 9:30." she had instructed. I thought it was too late to call her; she might be asleep. I did not like to wake her late at night because I was afraid it would scare her. All day Saturday we were busy as well.

About 6:00 p.m. that Saturday Bob went to the restaurant close by to get us some hushpuppies for supper. While he was gone I called my mother, but there was no answer. It wasn't terribly unusual, but I did not remember her telling me that she had a function at church and that would be the only place she could be this time of day. I called Bob on his cell phone and asked if he could swing by her house to see if she was at home. She only lived one mile from us so it wasn't long when Bob called me back.

"Yes her car is here." He said.

My sister and her family were at the coast where they have a park model trailer set up so I knew that she had no contact with her that day. Becky and Bill had left on Friday morning and her daughter had gone down that morning to be with them.

"Well, knock on the door Bob." I was a little demanding.

"Okay, but the morning paper is out here too." He said

I was getting sick to my stomach. Deep down I knew something had happened, why had I not checked on her earlier? I heard him knocking and knocking and calling her, but no answer came.

"Bob," I cried, "get her door key out of my car and try to open the door."

"Okay wait a minute!"

I could hear what was going on as he opened my car and looked in the holder where I kept her keys. Going back to the door, he tried and tried to unlock it but it would not unlock.

"Come home and get me Bob, right now!" I was so terrified I was screaming.

While he was on his way I changed clothes and tried to reach my sister. No one answered so I left her a frantic message that I could not get mother to the door.

I was already at the mailbox when Bob arrived and in a moment I found myself standing at her back door trying desperately to get in. The key would not work. I picked up a yard décor and broke the door window. Bob reached inside and unlocked the door and it swung open. I stood outside and asked him to go in first. I was frightened as I imagined what I might find.

Bob called for me. I ran inside and there lay my mother on the kitchen floor face down. The stove had apparently been grabbed on her way down and the eye was turned on. Bob checked her pulse, but I knew she was gone. She had been dead since the night before. I instantly called 911 and cried "My mother is dead; I have found my mother dead!"

I fell across my mother's body and sobbed like a baby. "What happened mother, what happened? " I cried over and over again. I hugged her lifeless body hoping to discover in some way the misery that invaded my mind. What had occurred? What happened to my Mom? Did her call last night reveal any desperation? Did she call me for help? Question after question flooded my thoughts while we waited for the sheriff and EMS.

I finally reached my sister a couple minutes later. They were in shock and grief stricken as well. They threw things together for the five hour trip home. There were questions to be answered and information needed as the medics arrived. Then the car from the funeral home arrived to carry her body to the morgue. It was apparent she was dead before she even hit the floor. By all indications it was probably her heart. She had been throwing up some five days earlier and looked as if she did not feel well the entire week. Apparently she died sometime after she called me at 8:45 p.m. and before 9:30

p.m. when she told me she was going to bed. Her bed had not been turned down and she still had her contacts in.

I could not believe my mother was gone. I had not been so grieved in all my life by a death. God comforted our souls through the days that were ahead and arrangements were made for Monday on Memorial Day.

"How much more can I endure, Lord?" I thought so often while I was alone that next week. *"Behold, O Lord; for I am in distress. My heart is troubled; mine heart is turned within me ... abroad the sword bereaveth, at home it is like death."* Lamentations 1: 20

My sister and I called each other every few hours it seemed and we would cry our eyes out with the pain. Oh, how we missed our mom, but God our Father had not forgotten us and he pulled us up on his awesome lap of comfort and slipped his everlasting arms around us. There we found the strength to face another day, one day at a time.

I remember a story of a young man whose wife had died leaving him with a three year old child to rear alone. He was so distraught and things looked so bleak. After the funeral of his beloved wife he went home that night and tried to sleep. He had put the child's bed next to his for comfort. During the night the child said, "Daddy, are you there? I can't see you, it is so dark in here." "Yes dear, daddy is here." He replied. Then the child asked, "Can you put you hand on me so I can feel you?"

Some times things get so dark we can not see God's presence and we do not understand the whys in life. We can't even see the evidence of what He is doing, but He is there! He cares and loves us so much and He has His hand on us whether we feel it or not. Trusting is the evidence of things not seen.

CHAPTER XXVIII

IN HIS EYES

⌣∶∾

James 1:2-3 (NJKV) *My brethren, count it all joy when ye fall into various trials, knowing this, that the testing of your faith worketh patience.*

It has been almost two years now since my mother's death. My sister and I have everything taken care of. There was much to do with getting her house ready to sell. After it sold, I was able to get some of our bills paid off, and get out of some financial despair. Although, I would not have had my mom to pass away, God provided through her estate, so I could stay home. He makes no mistakes!

It has been an eventful year of recovery, a year of reflection. I have had to deal with some things I had not anticipated like anger, impatience, frustration, and the list goes on just like all things we as humans have to deal with. I thought I had conquered those issues, but to my surprise they raised up their ugly heads once again. I still had the same sin nature all God's children are tainted with. As long as we live in this body we will sin.

I remembered the children of Israel when they were in the wilderness and had complained so often and did not seem to remember God's blessings and provision. He had brought them out of captivity, parted the Red Sea and done many wonders for them and they still complained, griped and sinned. But how much better am I? Had I forgotten how God had provided time and time again and still go my own way, complaining? I had not been any better than they. I can not be perfect, but I do not have to allow sin to rule me and allow it to ruin my life. As I have worked through my anger, impatience, rebellion, frustration and all the other junk I had been carrying for years, I realized one thing God was impressing on me found in Deuteronomy 8:2 & 3

"And thou shalt remember all the ways which the Lord thy God led thee these forty years in the wilderness, to humble thee, and to test thee, to know what was in thine heart, whether thou wouldest keep his commandments, or not. And he humbled thee, and suffered thee to hunger, and feed thee with manna, which thou knewest not, neither did their fathers know; that he might make thee know that man doth not live by bread only, but by every word that proceedeth out of the mouth of the Lord doth man live."

Walking with the Lord has truly been an amazing adventure and has taken me places I had not dreamed of before, but more importantly it has allowed me the opportunity to know Him in ways that others have not experienced. We have journeyed together through this life, and God has provided for me just like He did for the children of Israel in the wilderness, just like He promised. I have not arrived yet and probably will never reach the point that we are all capable of by fully trusting in our Lord and walking in His steps moment by moment, nor reach the point I would really like to reach. Walking with Him takes an amazing amount of faith. He has chosen for us to walk this way, by faith not by sight; it is the only thing that pleases Him. (Hebrews 11:6)

Kelly (a miracle) went to several interviews and was hired with the hospital system in Charlotte. She has had several promotions now and is very excited about her job. It was amazing that she was the only one hired for that position without a college degree among the other five that were hired at the same time. God supplied a job and she is not planning to return to college for the time being.

Our middle daughter, Brooke, (a miracle) has re-married and lives in Wilmington, North Carolina. She enjoys painting Christmas ornaments and paints other things as well. She has a creative talent and uses it well. She is a warm and sensitive young lady in who I am very proud to have as my daughter.

Amanda, our oldest, (a miracle) lives in Northridge, California with her husband, Dan. She is extremely happy working in her church as a children's coordinator. She is very talented and caring for people. I am very proud of all my girls. They have turned out well, and I am so blessed by them.

"If there is a single theme that emerges from the entirety of Scripture, it is this: Through relationship with God, man is finally capable of doing that which he was incapable of doing on his own. That's what walking in the Spirit is all about. And that's what character is all about...Character is the by – product of dependency...Character is the will to do what is right, as defined by God regardless of personal cost."(Andy Stanley, Louder than Words) (Sisters, Oregon: Multnomah, 2004), 35, 174-75

God is not interested in how long it takes, how far He has to send us or even what it cost if He has something to teach us. He is perfecting our character in each trial and test regardless of the cost. I had many wrong expectations in this life. I pray each day that I would give God praise for who He is, not for what I think He should be.

I can certainly say I grew closer to the Lord than I ever thought was possible. I also learned that God could handle my anger, rebellion and disappointments. Nothing surprised Him at all. I felt His loving arms about me and felt Him teaching me to accept myself with my failures, faults and my mistakes. I still have problems with all this so I know to brace myself for what's to come next.

I also knew that all these things that I had endured were not a waste, that God never waste anything. My experiences had taught me a lot about myself and helped me understand that God cares so much for me that He provided the grace I needed to go through the deep hurts I had encountered. I firmly believe that all my pains, hurts, experiences and trials are exactly what God had designed for my life so that I could grow in my faith and dependency upon Him daily. Certainly without them I still would be the same person I was forty years ago. In the end as I look back, I understand that God never uses anyone greatly until they are hurt deeply.

I don't know what the future holds, but I do know that **God makes no mistakes,** whatever happens.

HE MAKETH NO MISTAKE

My Father's way may twist and turn,
My heart may throb and ache,
But in my soul I'm glad I know,
He maketh no mistake.

My cherished plans may go astray,
My hopes may fade away,
But still I'll trust the Lord to lead,
For he doth know the way.

Tho night be dark and it may seem,
That day will never break,
I'll pin my faith, my all in Him,
He maketh no mistake.

There's so much now I cannot see,
My eyesight far too dim,
But come what may, I'll simply trust
And leave it all to Him.

For by and by the mist will lift,
And plain it all He'll make,
Through all the way, tho dark to me,
He made not one mistake.

Author Unknown

~:~

I CAN'T LIVE A DAY WITHOUT YOU

I could live life alone
And never feel the longings of my heart
The healing warmth of someone's arms
And I could live without dreams
And never know the thrill of what could be
With every star so far and out of reach
I could live with many things
And I could carry, but...I couldn't face my life tomorrow
Without Your hope in my heart I know

I can't live a day without You
Lord, there's no night and there's now morning
Without Your loving arms to hold me
You're the heartbeat of all I do
I can't live a day without you

I could travel the world
See all the wonders beautiful to me
They'd only make me think of You
And I could have all life offers
Riches that were far beyond compare
To grant my wish without a care
Oh, I could do anything
And I could carry on, oh yes
But if you weren't in at all...
Jesus, I live because You live
You're like the air I breathe
Oh Jesus, oh, I have because You give
You're everything to me Oh...
Avalon

Started reading this BOOK on January 4/2011
Finished on January 14, 2011.

Praise God for this sister my sister in the Lord. What a Life Testamony she and her husband with their three girls have Lived. We have to truly Trust God with all but Nothing Faith. This book is Truly The Meaning of how one can develope their Faith and Trust in God what an enjoyable reading. It keep me motivated to Continue reading as well as inspired through her Lifes Journey.

Printed in the United States
203351BV00001B/112-1026/P